UNSTUCK!

The 5 Factors of the
World's Highest-Performing Organisations

A Practical Handbook for CEOs and Leaders
who want to Accelerate the Performance of
their Organisation

MIKE ALAFACI

First Published in Australia 2025

By Michael Alafaci

www.mikealafaci.com

Please direct all enquiries to:

mike@mikealafaci.com

PRINT ISBN: 978-1-7638658-3-9

For Ken Katzenberger

Thank you for your professional, caring and fun style. You taught us how to be successful while taking care of each other and having fun along the way. You lived your own words, "Guys we want to be the best. Let's take our jobs seriously, but let's not take ourselves too seriously".

R.I.P. Ken.
You were and still are much loved and respected.

About the Author

Mike Alafaci is a senior business executive and management consultant. He has worked with some of the world's largest organisations on large-scale transformation and the development of high-performing leaders and teams.

He has lived and worked in Australia, the USA, Asia Pacific, Europe and the UK, leading regional and global teams. His teams consistently delivered results in the top 5% globally by being empowered to innovate, move quickly and work together with full accountability. And they had fun doing it!

Mike left his corporate career to help others be successful. In his own words, "I have seen too many people succeed in business by hurting others. It doesn't have to be like that. I want to help people be wildly successful in a way they can be proud of".

Foreword

I met Mike in 2004. He had recently returned from the USA after a stellar international career leading large sales and services teams with SAP (one of the world's largest software companies). At that time, I was in a national Human Resources and Organisational Development role for an ASX-listed, fast-growing tech company.

A respected colleague, who had collaborated with Mike when he was with SAP Australia, asked me to meet him. My colleague mentioned that Mike was now consulting and might be able to help our business. So, as a favour to my colleague, I met Mike.

It turned out to be one of the most fortuitous favours I have ever done.

Since then, Mike and I have achieved so much together and apart. What started as a supplier-client relationship grew into a co-collaboration relationship, a partnership in business, and a wonderful friendship. We have supported each other through births, deaths, marriages, many career highs, and a few lows.

In our first meeting, I asked Mike why he had decided to leave a company that had given him the opportunity to work across the world with some of the biggest companies on the planet. I had done some research and knew Mike had been very successful, and I had an idea of the pay packet he would have walked away from. I was pondering why someone would leave that kind of career opportunity and security, to strike out on their own mid-career and set up a small consulting business. I was caught between thinking he was very brave and a bit of a fool.

When I asked him why he was making this career change, he paused, looked me in the eye, and said something like, "I have seen too many people succeed by hurting others. It doesn't have to be this way. I want to help people be wildly successful in a way they can be proud of."

I immediately thought, this is someone I can work with, and who would be great for our business.

Mike's first consulting engagement with our business was not an easy one. I gave him a newly created sales team to coach. It was a small team of three: a senior salesperson with enormous potential but who was personally and professionally a bit of a mess, a former professional sportsperson new to the tech sector, and a junior salesperson who had no concept of how good they could be. We measured the improvement in the team's performance from the time Mike started working with them. The results were more than $1M in six months.

Since then, I have seen Mike work with many teams across a multitude of successful organisations and industry sectors. He has coached senior executives, CEOs, and Managing Directors, helping them to be more successful in both their professional and personal lives. I have watched him accelerate the performance of individuals, teams and organisations who he has worked for, and consulted to.

Unlike some consultants, Mike has kept himself relevant by stepping back into large and challenging corporate roles, helping teams and businesses turn around, become unstuck, and succeed. He is not just a consultant who coaches and consults based on years-old experience; he is a senior executive who has current, and firsthand knowledge of the challenges of leading large teams and divisions in complex organisations and markets.

Everyone in a leadership role feels stuck from time to time, and their organisations get stuck too. To get their organisation unstuck, leaders need to seek new ways of thinking and doing. If this is you, this practical book gives you easy frameworks to implement and new ideas to consider. If you are not feeling stuck right now but need a reminder of best practices, or confirmation that you and your organisation are on track to remain in flow, this book is also for you.

I had the honour of being a sounding board when Mike was building the concepts for this book and one of the first to read the completed manuscript. What I love about this book is that I have seen Mike put all these ideas into action. He has proven his concepts through trial and error, learning from both amazing and terrible leaders and deep research of what some of the highest performing organisations in the world do to accelerate their performance.

If you are driven to improve the performance of your organisation and achieve extraordinary results in a way you are proud of, this is a great book for you. I hope you gain as much value from it as I did.

Lindy MacPherson
Director APAC – Leader Experience Experts
Author – Lead with HEART

Who Is This Book For?

Firstly, it is for busy people. This book is brief so you can read it over a weekend and get started on Monday.

Secondly, this book is for organisations that need to get better results, faster. It is for large corporate, government, not-for-profit and also fast-growing organisations becoming stuck under the weight of their own success.

And thirdly, this book is for a certain type of leader. You may be a board member, CEO, executive or emerging leader, but you are a certain type. You are driven not just to make money (money is good by the way) but you are also driven to make a positive difference that you are proud of. That is what great reputations and legacy are made of. And at the end of our current role, our career and our life, that's what we will be remembered for—the difference (no matter how large or small) that we made using our talents and resources.

If this is you, welcome to a journey that will forever alter the trajectory of your leadership, the success of your organisation and the depth of your personal satisfaction.

Have fun reading this book. Then have more fun doing it!

Mike Alafaci

Introduction

Almost everyone in every organisation everywhere wants the same thing — to get results faster.

Many organisations are not getting results as fast as they want to. Individual contributors are frustrated by complexity, people and obstacles that slow their work down. Leaders who are under constant short-term pressure, are equally frustrated at their attempts to get people to achieve results faster.

There are 2 things in any organisation that lead to results: Strategy and Execution.

Most organisations are confident with their strategy. It is their execution that is holding them back. They are stuck, at least to some degree, in the way they execute. It seems that whatever they try — launching new initiatives; making cutbacks; setting new KPIs; restructures—it's a constant struggle to execute well enough to get the results they need.

Being stuck is frustrating. Becoming unstuck is highly satisfying and achievable.

Any organisation can become unstuck! And I can prove it. My proof is demonstrated by the world's high-performing organisations that exist in almost every industry, in both the private and public sectors.

So how do these high-performing organisations move faster than their peers? How do they produce results quarter after quarter, and continue to lead their industries?

The answer is not better people. They have access to the same talent pool as everyone else. It's not that they have better technology. Everyone has access to the same technology. And it's not that they have better funding or a better strategy.

The answer is that they execute better than their peers by executing differently. On the surface they execute like their peers, but when you look under the hood there are small differences that have a big impact on their speed and results.

A Different Approach

A growing number of leaders are realising they need a different approach to executing for results. The good news is that there is a different approach, and it is being used by the world's high-performing organisations.

As a management consultant who has worked in the USA, UK, EU, Australia and New Zealand, I have spent my career fascinated by the things that separate high-performing organisations from all others. I asked myself questions like, how did they launch products and services that leapfrogged their peers? How did they create breakthroughs in their industry that others now follow? How did they get people to commit and work so well together to achieve those results? What did they do differently? And how did they do it?

Over the years I tested what I had learned and got results in my own leadership roles. I shared this experience with other leaders, and I consulted to organisations who also enjoyed the satisfaction and results that followed.

In the leadup to this book, I spent years researching many of the world's high-performing organisations (and organisations that were stuck and not performing as well as they wanted) to understand what they do differently and how they do it. I found a set of practices that high-performing organisations share. These practices formed the 5 Factors of high-performing organisations.

This book is my effort to share my experience and my research. It reveals the 5 Factors of Execution that the world's high-performing organisations leverage to get results. It not only shows you what, and how, but at the end of the book, there is a roadmap to get started in your own organisation, and a tool to measure how your organisation currently scores on the 5 Factors.

How hard, expensive and risky is this?

Most management consultants will tell you that you need to invest upfront to gain rewards later. This means it will hurt before it gets better. I am NOT one of those consultants. The approach outlined in this book is cost neutral and designed to generate results immediately. It can be applied at a pace and depth that suits your organisation's culture and current situation.

Does it require effort? Sure, but a better question is: What do we need to do differently to get different results, faster?

The 5 Factors of High-Performing Organisations

The 5 Factors in this book are found in many of the world's high-performing organisations. But what exactly is a high-performing organisation?

There are many lists that rank organisations. The Forbes Global 2000 ranks organisations by Financial Performance. Fortune's 100 Best Companies to Work For ranks organisations by Employee Satisfaction. The Times World's Best Companies rank performance by market capitalisation, net promoter score, and environmental, social and governance factors.

The problem is that none of these lists is a reliable indicator of high-performance. For example, the most popular ranking is financial performance. Investors might value financial performance rankings, but financial performance alone is not a true indicator of the health and subsequent performance of an organisation.

Financial metrics are easily manipulated, often at the expense of other metrics like employee engagement, customer satisfaction and the organisation's ability to continue to innovate and grow. Any executive manager can lower costs with offshoring, deferring, or lowering costs. This works in the short-term, but over time the health of a business weakens. For this reason, financial performance metrics alone are not a reliable indicator of performance—especially if an organisation is intending to reinvent, grow or achieve significant outcomes.

The goal of any organisation is to satisfy customers, attract the best talent and produce a return on capital (profits for corporations or outcomes for governments). These 3 fundamental metrics provide a more reliable indicator of performance.

- Customer Satisfaction
- Employee Engagement
- Financial Performance

The high-performing organisations studied for this book score highly on all 3 of these metrics. Conversely, most organisations that underperform often have only one of these metrics in their sights— financial performance. We could blame the stock market for its relentless pressure to produce short-term profits, but that doesn't explain how the world's high-performing organisations manage to score highly on all three.

One of the reasons high-performing organisations score highly on all three is a deeply held belief that all

3 metrics are important to their success. And there is a good business reason: All 3 metrics are interconnected —they build momentum over time in a sustainable cycle. The cycle goes something like this: Engaged and empowered employees are more productive; they try harder and drive innovation in products and services. Innovation leads to operational efficiency, lower costs and a better customer experience. Loyal customers drive revenue growth. Revenue growth enables pricing power and further investment in innovation. A cycle like this keeps an organisation evolving to create more value for sustained high-performance.

How they made the list of high-performing organisations

The organisations selected had high scores on all 3 metrics of **employee, customer** and **financial** but also had a positive impact on their **industry**. An example of industry is the Automotive Industry. High-performing organisations whether Private, Government or Not-for-Profit sectors were selected for the impact on their industry, moving it forward and adding more value than others.

An example of industry impact is the Ford Motor Company's release of the first mass-produced car, the Model T in 1908. It had a profound impact, revolutionising transportation and manufacturing processes.

High-performing organisations make a positive impact on their industries every day that don't necessarily make world headlines.

High-Performing Organisations

A high-performing organisation is an organisation that strives to and scores highly on all 4 metrics of employee, customer, financial and industry.

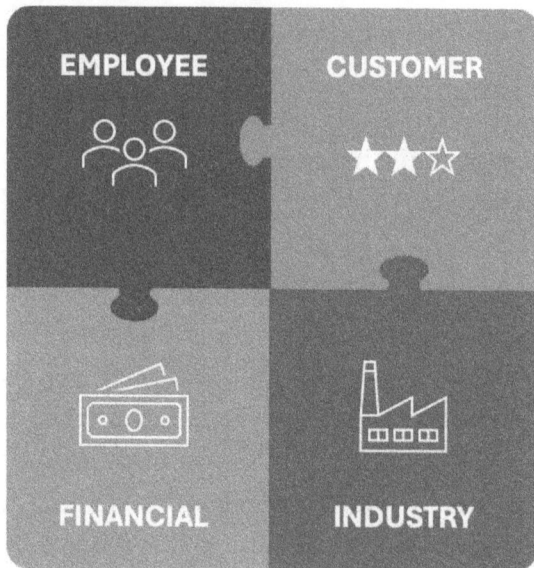

The Research Approach

Organisations were selected with high scores in customer, employee, financial results and impact on their industry.

Measures included:
- Customer Net Promoter Score (NPS)
- Customer retention and churn rates, customer spend levels
- Employee Satisfaction and eNPS
- Employee sentiment on social media platforms such as Glassdoor
- Financial growth, profit and enterprise value
- Examples of impact in their industry with products, services and influence on peers.

This data was assessed over 5, 10 and 20-year spans to current day and cross checked against various sources.

The Research Question

When these organisations were at their best, what exactly did they do to achieve such remarkable results and impact?

How did they think, act and lead their organisations? Why did they do better than their peers in the same industry with the same resources?

The organisations were then studied to find common practices that led to their high-performance. This data came from publications, interviews on record, press releases and many other sources that are publicly available.

The Findings

Upon analysing the data, several common practices emerged in each organisation. Regardless of industry or sector, strong and clear execution of these common practices were correlated with their ability to execute and generate high-performance and results.

The common practices found in each organisation formed the 5 Factors. These factors apply to any organisation in any industry and sector whether private, government or not-for-profit.

The 5 Factors

The 5 Factors found in high-performing organisations.

Factor #1
Hands-on Leadership is a leader's ability to engage and be visible in the operation with employees and customers, to hold a level of domain knowledge, encourage input and debate from all levels, set direction and empower people to be successful by removing obstacles and trusting them with the authority they need to do their job.

Factor #2
Purpose-Led Culture is an organisation's ability to create commitment, effort and engagement, both inside and outside their organisation, on the "reason we exist".

Factor #3
Customer-Centricity is an organisation's strategic and cultural orientation toward its customers. The ability to prioritise and create customer value while achieving returns and outcomes for the organisation.

Factor #4
Fully Empowered People is an organisation's ability to remove unnecessary obstacles, complexity and wasted effort, and to empower people with clear direction, authority, autonomy and accountability.

Factor #5
Cross-Team Collaboration is an organisation's ability to remove silos and to create alignment across teams that contribute to the achievement of the organisation's strategic objectives.

On the surface, these 5 Factors don't seem any different from what most companies say they do. And that's true. The difference is in how well they are executed. The high-performing organisations described in this book execute these 5 Factors exceptionally well, as you will see in the upcoming chapters.

DISCLAIMERS

Some people may be offended!

Disclaimer #1
You don't have to like them to learn from them.
   The organisations referenced in this book are here for you to learn from. You may not like them, their products or their leaders but that isn't the point. We don't have to like someone to learn from them—especially if they are successful. Just as one professional sporting team analyses video of another team, this book is an opportunity to gain insights into how some of the world's high-performing organisations execute the 5 Factors to achieve the results they achieve.

Disclaimer #2

Some of the organisations are controversial.

Amazon's past labour practices come to mind. However, most recently they have taken this seriously and made significant improvements. Regardless, it is Amazon's undeniable success and past behaviour we can learn from. Specifically, how they leveraged the 5 Factors to set the standard on customer-centricity and purpose to achieve the results they are known for.

Tesla and Elon Musk are also controversial. Musk's controversial behaviour and opinions, Tesla's Autopilot accidents, its labour practices and resistance to unionisation in a highly unionised industry brings Tesla's future into question.

You may not agree with their current behaviour, but their past success is the thing to learn from and use for yourself. Musk's ability to lead people to willingly achieve amazing results at Telsa and SpaceX is undeniable. SpaceX's groundbreaking achievements in aerospace raise the question of why larger, established industry leaders could not have done this first. Tesla set the precedent for electric vehicles (EVs), causing traditional manufacturers to follow, pushing EVs into the mainstream, expediting sustainable transport and energy ecosystems that set the standard for all others.

Their very real high scores on customer, employee and financial metrics, their impact on industry and their past achievements make them worthy of review.

How they did it is the question.

Disclaimer #3

Some organisations are polarising.

You love them or you hate them. Apple comes to mind. Their products are not as open as Microsoft or Google's. Apple control everything on their products from hardware to software. Some people appreciate it, and some hate it. Another criticism is that some people say Apple is not as innovative without Steve Jobs. When Jobs was alive Apple executed on the 5 Factors better, faster and with more impact than most organisations. It's hard to know what Jobs would be doing today, but Apple executes even better now than when Jobs was alive. Apple is 6 times larger than when Jobs was alive and is in the top 3 largest, most profitable organisations on the planet. Apple's execution of the 5 Factors, its impact on industry and consistent high scores on customer, employee and financial metrics is worthy of review.

Disclaimer #4

Change is the only constant. Nobody is perfect.

At one point in time all organisations referenced here were high-performing examples of 5 Factor Organisations. However, some have since lost their way, some may yet lose their way, and others have even found their way back.

There are many reasons organisations lose their way (maybe the subject of another book), but the most common reasons are:

- Leadership hubris, bred by success (leaders becoming overly self-confident and dismissive of advice, potential problems and criticisms that matter)
- Flawed strategy
- Neglecting the 5 Factors that earned them their success in the first place

The point is this: Each high-performing organisation achieved remarkable results at one point in time by executing well on the 5 Factors. How they executed the 5 Factors is the subject of this book.

Disclaimer #5
The organisations referenced are not an exhaustive list.
The research summarised in this book was not intended to be a large-scale data analysis. It is in-depth research on high-performance practices. The goal was to compare organisations to identify common practices that contributed to their high-performance across all metrics (customer, employee, financial and impact on their industry).

The 5 Factor Model contains practices that are common enough to be used in any industry with its constraints and opportunities.

The Organisations Studied
There were over 20 organisations studied that represent many of the world's high-performing organisations. The most prominent high-performing

organisations studied include Starbucks, Johnson & Johnson, Apple, LEGO, Best Buy, PepsiCo, Tesla, Disney, SAP, Marriott, Microsoft, Whole Foods, Virgin, In-N-Out Burger, Netflix, SpaceX, Berkshire Hathaway, Amazon, Hilton, Facebook (Meta) and Costco. There were other organisations studied that represent examples of poor execution on the 5 Factors and the negative impact on their performance.

The high-performing organisations share some other achievements. They rank in the world's top 100 most valuable brands and have for many years and their market capitalisation is close to the top of their industry. For example, Starbucks is the second most valuable fast-food restaurant in the world. Apple, Amazon and Microsoft are well-known for their market capitalisation. Tesla has the highest market capitalisation in the automotive industry—it is higher than the next 4 largest automotive organisations combined. Marriott is number one in its industry. SAP is the world's 50th most valuable company, but the third largest software company by sales. And Costco is the second largest supermarket chain. I could bore you silly with more statistics, but you get the idea.

These high-performing organisations are in different industries but share common practices. They are constantly evolving and striving to execute the 5 Factors, sometimes better and sometimes worse than they would like. But their impact on industry and performance scores on customer, employee and financial performance speak for themselves.

How Does Your Organisation Score?

During my research, leaders wanted to know how their organisation scored on the 5 Factors. In response, I developed an assessment tool to measure how well an organisation is executing on the 5 Factors. It provides an overall performance score, a score on each factor and then disaggregated scores to reveal specific gaps and opportunities in each factor across geography and department. The tool is called the 5 Factor Assessment Model of Execution (F.A.M.E.). There is a short chapter devoted to it at the end of the book.

A Note on Environmental, Social & Governance (ESG)

ESG, while important, is assumed but not covered in this book for 2 reasons: The first is that ESG continues to evolve with different requirements on different continents. When it matures, ESG will balance an organisation's impact on the world and its need for financial return. The second reason it is not covered is that ESG will be viewed as a fundamental responsibility (like safety). It will become a standard part of business planning for capital allocation, business models and strategy.

A note on how the 5 Factors relate to strategy & execution

As mentioned earlier, there are two things that contribute to high-performance in any organisation: strategy and execution. For decades, MBA programs and business books have focused on the importance of strategy. Strategy became the focus of leaders, while execution was left to middle managers and frontliners. To some degree execution was confused with being "tactical" or doing work that was a waste of a leader's time. This trend led to unintended negative consequences in many organisations.

The first unintended consequence is leaders becoming disconnected from the knowledge they need to embed strategy and get it executed. Their focus on strategy and pressure to focus on numbers means they hold domain knowledge of "strategic" elements like industry trends, markets, stakeholders and financial performance, but they have lost "execution" knowledge of their products, services, customers and employees. This robs them of the detail and influence required to embed strategy in operation. A sure sign of this is when they attempt to implement new initiatives that slowly fail to produce the results they need.

In this environment, it is common to see employees disengage, while productivity and customer satisfaction decline and then the inevitable impact on financial results. When this happens, it is common for leaders set more conservative strategic goals (so they don't fail) and to place more controls on people to achieve the goals (which further slows them down). Ironically the focus on strategy and the disconnect from execution can lead to a less ambitious strategy and even slower execution and results.

The 5 Factors used by the world's high-performing organisations are grounded in both strategic and operational knowledge. This allows them to lead execution with greater confidence for better results, faster.

If an organisation can't get its execution right, it doesn't matter how great its strategy is. But with solid execution, leaders can confidently set ambitious goals, leverage new technologies, talent and new business models with a much higher chance of achieving better results, faster.

Execution is an Executive responsibility. The 5 Factor Model empowers Executives to drive execution with confidence, to align, embed and action their strategy to deliver high-performance and results.

The Bottom Line

- Becoming unstuck and accelerating performance begins with a focus all 4 metrics of employee, customer, financial and industry
- The world's high-performing organisations all share common practices or the 5 Factors.
- High-performance is correlated with strong execution of the 5 factors in these organisations.
- High-performing organisations prioritise both strategic and operational knowledge to drive execution of their strategy.
- Many global leadership surveys reveal that leaders are less aware of the barriers to execution than their workers.
- Your organisation's execution can be measured using the Five Factor Assessment Model of Execution (F.A.M.E.) tool.
- Any organisation in any industry can replicate the 5 Factors.
- Executing the 5 Factors starts with Factor #1 Hands-on Leadership.

Factor #1
Hands-On Leadership

Getting people to execute well is what separates the world's high-performing organisations from all others. Unfortunately, many organisations have a gap between strategy and execution. The gap is between the leaders who set the strategy and the workers who execute it.

This gap goes both ways. Workers say that leaders don't understand what they do or what they need. Leaders say workers don't appreciate the constraints and reasons behind the strategy.

More concerning are studies show that only 1 in 7 workers (15% of the people who execute the strategy) can name only 1 of the strategic goals their leaders had set. And of those people, half of them admitted they were not committed to achieve the goal, nor were they held accountable for progress against the goals.

It is no wonder that execution is a big problem for executives. If most people don't know where the goal posts are, how can they possibly kick a goal? And if the small number of people who can see the goal posts don't care about kicking a goal and are not held accountable, chances of winning the game are significantly reduced.

So, who's responsibility is the gap between strategy and execution?

In a sporting team, the responsibility sits firmly with the team coach—the owner of the strategy. In an organisation the team coach and owner of the strategy is the CEO and their executive team.

The problem is that many CEOs and their executive teams are disconnected from the people in the operation. Many leaders recognise the importance of staying connected to the operation, its people and customers. They value the wealth of knowledge available to them. Yet many are isolated by information overload, time constraints and structures that prevent direct access and information flow.

The solution to closing the gap and becoming more connected is to become more hands-on. The world's high-performing organisations have hands-on leaders at every level of leadership. They obsess over execution as much as strategy.

Being a hands-on leader positions CEOs and boards to avoid the mistakes of clinging to old business models until it is too late, failing to adapt new technology and not continually improving their organisations effectiveness. It also makes it easier to attract the best talent, leverage new technology and implement new business models to achieve exceptional results. In short, being hands-on is a major factor in accelerating execution.

Hands-on leadership does not take any extra time. It is highly influential and well-received by people. It melts resistance, increases engagement and significantly increases the success of leadership initiatives and strategies. And it is the first factor leveraged by leaders of the world's highest-performing organisations.

The Elements of Hands-on Leadership
1- Understands & Connects

They hold domain knowledge of their business and the understand what their people do and their challenges. They are engaged in data and detail required to drive initiatives that will be seen as relevant and actionable by those in the operation. They understand the operation, employee and customer needs. And they are visible and active in the operation to connect, listen to and share ideas, and to motivate others at all levels.

2 - Leads & Empowers

They set clear direction and goals that are achievable and relevant to people who execute them. They remove obstacles, trust people and grant them authority to make decisions on how they work to achieve results. They encourage ideas and debate, not compliance. The best idea wins not the loudest or most senior opinion.

3 - Practices Empathy

They view empathy as a business skill. They seek to understand employee and customer needs. They communicate their understanding of employee and customer needs in a clear and accurate way that directly increases their influence, credibility and has a direct impact on business results. They take action to manage and meet employee and customer needs.

These 3 elements of Hands-on Leadership work together to get people to execute for better results, faster.

1
The Hands-On Leader

Hands-on leaders have an advantage. Think about any of the world's greatest organisations. They were built by hands-on leaders. Now think about great organisations that lost their way. Hands-on leaders are the ones who turned them around.

Accelerating execution and results starts at the top. While costs are part of the solution, too many CEOs turn to layoffs to protect profits and restructures to stimulate growth. These strategies address the symptom but not the cause. They achieve short-term results, but damage employee engagement, forward momentum and ongoing profitability. After layoffs and restructures, most organisations are left weaker.

A growing number of leaders are beginning to realise they need a different approach to accelerating execution and results.

Hands-on leaders are better positioned to make changes that strengthen an organisation, not weaken it. Rather than across-the-board cuts, they cut unnecessary projects, budgets and even before that, they cut red tape, rules, processes and anything that is unnecessarily slowing their organisation down. They lower friction to move faster.

Moving faster requires a clear view of exactly what is slowing you down. The biggest problem for CEOs, boards and executive teams is getting an unfiltered, balanced view of what will speed up results.

A CEO is often the most isolated person in the organisation. Their team rarely give them unfiltered information. Some CEOs are hesitant to ask questions below their direct reports for fear of looking incompetent or out of touch. Others just don't have a way to uncover this information. As organisations grow it is common to see an increasing gap between leadership and the operation, its people and customers.

The key to closing this gap and gaining invaluable insights is to become hands-on; getting closer to the operation, its people and customers. When a CEO is hands-on, it breeds a hands-on culture through the leadership ranks.

The last thing you want is hands-off people below you giving you poor advice. I have seen a lot of senior functional leaders masquerading as experts when in fact they have no idea what is going on in their team or business. Their strategy is flimsy and developed in isolation from the people with operational knowledge required to execute it. They bluff their way through meetings with the CEO and Board, who, if they are also hands-off, have no choice but to believe them.

Numbers: The path to isolation

A common trap is to become numbers driven. It's like counting your chips at the poker table instead of concentrating on playing the actual game. Business is like poker: if you run out of money it is game over. But counting chips isn't a skill that wins at poker. It is focussing on playing the actual game. It is getting into the detail of what is going on, how the players are playing, what cards you hold and how you are executing your game strategy. Counting chips too often will distract you from playing, enjoying and winning the game.

Leaders who are obsessed with numbers often live in their office. I fell into this trap early in my career. I realised I was losing touch with the details of the operation, its products, people and customers, and the very details needed to confidently direct resources and efforts to get the best possible results.

Hands-on leaders are rarely in their office

You never see a start-up CEO or a turnaround CEO driving an organisation from their office. You will see them in every functional unit spending time with leaders, frontliners and customers, learning and contributing ideas. They are not worried about being seen to have all the answers, they play a facilitator role. They meet with their people at all levels to solve problems, remove obstacles, offer support, and encourage ideas to drive the creation of value and results. Leaders of the world's high-performing organisations do this.

Elon Musk might be controversial, but he is an effective hands-on CEO. When Tesla was struggling to increase production, Musk moved his desk onto Tesla's factory floor to better understand and help solve production issues. In his own words he said:

> "I think it's important for a leader to be at the front lines. The challenges are in ramping up production...It's about being in the factory and understanding where the issues are, and I want the very opposite of being up in an ivory tower; I want to be in the middle of the battle, and so that means putting my desk in the middle of the factory". [18]

Remove obstacles and empower people to act

Being a hands-on leader is not just about being visible in the operation. It is about getting involved and connecting with people to understand what they need, and constantly looking for obstacles to remove that are holding people and the organisation back. Cutting obstacles before cutting people wherever possible strengthens and accelerates execution and performance.

Hands-on leaders invite people to speak up about what works and what doesn't. But they need to be encouraged to speak up. People won't speak up unless the CEO or their leader makes it clear that all feedback and ideas are welcome.

Elon Musk followed up with this email to Tesla staff:

"If there is something you think should be done to make Tesla execute better or allow you to look forward to coming to work more, please send a note".[19]

Tesla employees are empowered to make decisions. This is because strategy and goals are not developed in isolation. They are developed in consultation with the people who execute the strategy. People know what is expected, why it is important and that they are accountable and invested in the outcome.

Hands-on leaders trust their people to do their jobs. And if people don't do their jobs, hands-on leaders hold them accountable by providing support or managing them out.

Elon Musk is only one of many examples of well-known hands-on leaders. Many of the world's most successful leaders have been hands-on. Walt Disney, Henry Ford, Steve Jobs, Bill Gates, Richard Branson, Larry Ellison, Jeff Bezos, Mark Zuckerberg, have all achieved incredible results from their hands-on style. Can you imagine any of them achieving what they did without being hands-on?

Admittedly these are all founders. You may be thinking, what about non-founder, professional CEOs?

Many professional CEOs have picked up where the founders left off or have stepped in to turn organisations around by being hands-on. Indra Nooyi, former PepsiCo CEO, transformed the bloated behemoth with her hands-on leadership.

Hubert Joly's hands-on approach resulted in Best Buy's remarkable turnaround. Mary Barra, CEO of General Motors, is transforming the automaker with her hands-on approach. Howard Schultz was known for transforming Starbucks into a global brand with his hands-on approach in store design, customer experience and attention to strategic operations. Satya Nadella's hands-on involvement in product, partnering, customer needs and employee input has transformed Microsoft after previously losing its focus on and missing many tech industry trends.

Keep an eye out for the next turnaround CEO who takes an organisation to new levels of success and performance. I guarantee they will also be hands-on.

Hands-on or Micromanager

Hands-on leadership is not micromanagement. It is often confused with micromanagement, which is excessive control of every detail and decision. Micromanagers hold people responsible but do not give them matching authority. Micromanagers operate from a place of fear and anxiety. They don't trust people and they fear failure so exercise over control. In contrast, hands-on leaders operate with quiet confidence, empathy and emotional maturity. They trust people but are smart about how they trust.

Hands-on leaders become involved in their business to understand and support people. They provide strategy, expectations and guidance—not from a distance that people don't respect—but from direct connection with and knowledge of their people, business and customers.

They empower people by giving them responsibility and matching authority, then they trust people to do their jobs. When people underperform, they hold them to account and either manage or move them on. Having conversations to manage performance is significantly easier with a hands-on leadership approach. A leader starting from a place of connection, clear expectations, support and trust will find that people will quickly correct their performance or elect to move themselves.

Micromanager or Hands-off

Micromanagement has an opposite partner that is just as bad: Hands-off leadership. People led by a hands-off leader often lack direction and are unclear about goals. The result is misaligned teams and conflicting agendas. Hands-off leaders shy away from giving people feedback or guidance needed to perform at their best or to be held accountable. Hands-off leaders describe themselves as "strategic" and not "tactical". They are not being "strategic", they are being lazy.

Hands-off leaders are often disconnected with what is going on in the business. They rollout strategies and initiatives that are met with resistance at the operational level because they are not appropriate, not practical or not understood. They blame people for not behaving as they should, yet they don't understand why people resist their initiatives and what their people actually need to get results.

Hands-off and micromanagement are at two opposite ends of the spectrum. Neither is good. They are weak and lazy forms of leadership.

Too hard, too soft and just right

Hands-on leadership is right in the middle of the spectrum. It gives people control and flexibility, but it is also crystal clear about setting expectations. It empowers and manages performance. It's done by managers getting involved in the detail and the data, communicating with empathy and influence, clearing obstacles and empowering people by giving them the tools and trust to get the job done.

Hands-on leadership is best understood by its impact on people.

The following illustrates how most people at all levels describe working for hands-on leaders compared to micromanagers and hands-off leaders.

Hands-on leaders	Hands-off / Micromanagers
You understand your people, the value they create and the challenges they have.	You don't really understand what your people do or the challenges they face.
You often visit the operation, engage with people to contribute, learn and to share updates that engage and motivate people.	You are rarely seen in your people's workplace below your direct reports. You rarely have conversations with workers below your direct reports.
You are aware of operational problems. You contribute ideas and you encourage others to offer ideas.	You are involved in the operation only when you need to control decisions and impose your ideas.
You understand your organisation's products, customer needs and operation. You are respected because your vision aligns with the people responsible for executing it.	You have little understanding of your organisation's product value, customer needs and operation. You are viewed as a numbers-focused leader who is disconnected from the organisation's core business.

The organisation's strategy is relevant to the workers who execute it.	Workers don't understand or believe in the strategy.
You manage to balance customer, employee and shareholder needs.	You are focussed only on your bosses and your success.
You are constantly looking for obstacles to remove and ways to empower your people to get results.	You create bottlenecks in decisions and process that hinder productivity and stifle innovation.
You set clear goals for your people that are achievable and focused on results.	You set goals but are more interested in controlling the process than allowing people to achieve results.
You enable people by giving them responsibility and equal authority.	You control people by giving them responsibility but lower authority.
You trust people to do their job. You ensure they have the knowledge, tools and resources to be successful.	You don't really trust people to do their job. You limit their resources and control.
You let people decide how work is done.	You monitor every step of how work is done.

You are comfortable discussing people's performance holding people to account.	You are uncomfortable discussing people's performance and don't hold people to account.
You treat mistakes as learning opportunities to lift performance. You coach people to support their growth and results.	You punish mistakes by adding more controls that slow performance. You expect people to work it out and do not coach them or get involved to help.
They trust you and your motivations. They will go above and beyond for you.	They don't trust your motivations. They do the minimum to keep their job.

Hands-on leadership flows down

Hands-on leadership is for all leaders in an organisation. It starts at the top and flows through the executive team, middle management and all the way to the front-line. Its elements apply to the CEO and the front-line supervisor.

Apple, one of the world's largest high-performing organisations is an example of hands-on leadership at every level. At Apple there are no general managers. All leaders from the executive team down are involved in the detail. They hold domain knowledge at least 2 levels below those who report to them. The reason is best described by Apple themselves:

"It's easier to get the balance right between an attention to costs and the value added to the user experience when the leaders making decisions are those with deep expertise in their areas rather than general managers being held accountable primarily for meeting numerical targets".[20]

Hands-on managers mentor their staff. They split their time using their expertise and mentoring others to grow their expertise.

Poor performing staff are the often a result of hands-off managers. You see this all the time, for example, retail sales staff who stand around doing nothing instead of helping customers, or sales staff who know less about a product than the customer. These people have not been shown exactly what is expected or how to do their job, nor are they held accountable.

Hands-off managers not only have under-performing staff, they are disconnected and don't see poor results coming. They use blunt instruments and sweeping changes to correct results, like laying off staff across the board using a spreadsheet, instead of proactively boosting performance and results by being involved and connected like hands-on managers.

An isolated CEO means an isolated Board

Isolated CEOs often live in their office, obsessing over numbers rather than leading value creation and empowering the organisation. They drop in with strategies built in isolation that people cannot and will not get behind because they are disconnected from the operation and the customer. A CEO who is out of touch with employees, the operation and customer value creation is a risk to the board.

Boards need hands-on CEOs. A hands-on CEO is better positioned to inform the board of exactly what is going on in the organisation. They can produce solid plans for value creation based on knowledge of operational and strategic considerations. They can report solid progress in qualitative and quantitative terms. And they can more accurately anticipate risks, impacts and trends down the track.

Their combination of strategic and high-level operational knowledge is credible. It wins the confidence of investors, customers and employees. Combined with skilful use of empathy, it positions them strongly to handle the inevitable crises that can damage the brand or market share.

Being hands-on doesn't waste time—it saves time

Remarkably, hands-on CEOs and leaders have more time for themselves. They also waste less of other people's time. They don't tie themselves and others up in approvals and unnecessary meetings. They devolve authority and accountability which gives them more time to spend on things that move the organisation forward.

They have more time to set shared goals that unite and align the organisation. They have time to stay involved with functional leaders and their teams, contributing ideas and being the champion of collaboration and performance.

Being hands-on doesn't mean being overly tactical or doing jobs below your area of responsibility. It is simply connecting strategy with operational involvement and guidance. It is a reallocation of a leader's time.

A hands-off leader can easily spend all their time analysing spreadsheets, reporting upward, and sitting in unnecessary meetings to approve things they don't need to approve.

Contrast that with a hands-on CEO and leadership team who spend time listening to and learning from employees in the operation, challenging ideas and leaning into problems. This way of operating gives them great insight to steer the organisation with confidence.

The role of hands-on leadership in the 5 Factors

Hands-on leadership is the essential foundation for the successful implementation of the remaining four. A purpose-led culture (Factor #2) requires a deep understanding of your people, your customers and your operation. It requires empathy and detailed knowledge obtained from being hands-on to articulate and integrate purpose for results.

Creating customer-centricity (Factor #3) requires a hands-on connection with front line employees to understand customer needs and the operation's ability to deliver them.

Fully empowered people (Factor #4) depend on hands-on leaders. They receive clear guidance, support, feedback and input for problem-solving. They are encouraged to share ideas and are trusted to make decisions and be accountable.

Cross-team collaboration (Factor #5) need hands-on leaders who create and manage shared goals that encourage people to work together not against each other. They create a collaborative environment with regular cross-team progress meetings against shared goals.

How you can become more hands-on

Whether you have drifted away from being hands-on or have joined an organisation where you need to acquire industry or product knowledge, it is never too late to learn to become more hands-on as a leader.

5 things you can do immediately to become more hands-on

1. **Become more connected and less isolated.**
Reassess where you are spending your time. Be visible and be involved. You can learn more in a few days of listening to front liners than you can from months of spreadsheets and executive meetings in

isolation. Hands-on leaders delegate authority. It helps your people move faster, take ownership and it saves you a lot of time. The time you save allows you to spend more time connecting with and gaining insight into your people, operation and customers to confidently direct value-creation that generates results.

2. Set direction, then trust people to do their job.

Hands-on leaders set clear direction then trust people to do their part. Give people more control with matching accountability to make decisions within their area of expertise and accountability. It helps your people move faster, take ownership and it saves you a lot of time. Coach your managers to be more hands-on.

3. Remove "unnecessary" obstacles.

Encourage people to speak up if there are obstacles holding them back and making work harder than it should be. Reverse the trend to add rules and complexity. Start identifying and removing complexity. Expect great things from people so they can do great things. Raise the bar but lower approval levels by delegating authority to those best positioned to make decisions and be accountable.

4. Build influence and engagement with empathy.

Start using your knowledge and understanding of people and the operation to build empathy, rapport, influence and engagement by showing that you understand people and what they need. Communicate with people about their work and yours. Create a connection and understanding between the front line and the boardroom. Retain ownership of your vision and culture while becoming a highly influential leader powered by your hands-on insights into your people and customers and your passion for the business.

5. Say NO to a lot more things

By saying no you can be more hands-on and able to focus on the major goals and outcomes. How did a hands-on leader like Steve Jobs run such an enormous organisation while staying across every major project, developing vision and strategy and contributing to product design elements?

The answer, in Jobs' own words is, "Deciding what not to do is as important as deciding what to do"[21].

Jobs believed that focus wasn't about saying yes, it was about saying NO to a hundred things so you could focus on the few things that were important. Saying NO is hard to do and hard to hear. People will complain, but you are not there to please everyone who wants something from you. You are there to get results by focussing on what matters.

The Bottom Line

- Moving faster requires a clear view of exactly what is slowing you down.
- As organisations grow it is common to see an increasing gap between leadership and the operation, its people and customers.
- The gap often shows up between strategy and execution where execution does not meet expectations.
- CEOs and leaders of the world's high-performing organisations obsess over execution as much as strategy.
- The key to closing this gap and gaining invaluable insights is to become actively connected to their people, operation and customers to sync strategy with the reality of the business, resources, operation, customer and industry trends.
- Hands-on leaders accelerate their own and their people's productivity by setting clear direction then trusting people to do their jobs with greater authority and matching accountability.
- They seek to remove unnecessary obstacles and complexity.
- Hands-on leadership is for all leaders in an organisation.
- Hands-on leadership is the foundation for the remaining 4 factors.

2

The Smartest Person in the Room

As a leader, has it ever crossed your mind that you may be holding people back?

Most CEOs and senior executives are highly intelligent people. That's why they are there, but it doesn't mean they have to be the smartest person in the room. Taking on that role either through a sense of responsibility or self-importance can hold other people back from contributing and engaging.

Nobody likes working for someone who thinks they are the smartest person in the room. You know them, the ones that always know best. They make all the decisions and shut down anything that challenges their ideas.

Hands-on leaders leverage the power of the knowledge held in their people.

CEOs and senior executives don't need to have all the answers. They have people for that. Henry Ford was rumoured to say he didn't have all the answers, but he knew who to ask to find them. That is a display of humility, intelligence, and maturity.

The Best Ideas Win

A leader's role is not to make all the decisions or to have all the best ideas (how could they anyway?). Their role is to create an environment that encourages people to share ideas, debate them and allow the best ideas to win.

The more you encourage your people to share their ideas, the more they will take ownership of the change required to implement them. The more autonomy you give people to run with ideas, the faster your organisation will get results.

People Hold the Answer to Becoming Unstuck

An essential part of increasing performance is gaining input and knowledge from the bottom up. There is a wealth of knowledge and detail that only frontline workers have. CEOs and their executive teams need this detail to steer the organisation effectively.

As an executive coach, I have seen the alternative many times: intelligent people with privileged access to information and position think they are the smartest people in the room. They overrule people to get their own way often to soothe their own anxiety about undesirable outcomes. This kind of environment leads to poor decisions by senior leaders. It almost always lowers respect and engagement from the people who are overruled, and it lowers the leader's ability to truly influence and inspire people to do their best work. This is not how modern leaders lead or how employees want to be led.

The Bigger Person, Not the Smartest

The CEOs and senior executives in the world's high-performing organisations take on the role of the bigger person in the room, not the smartest. They carry their authority with responsibility, experience and a duty of care to the people they lead. Being the smartest person in the room is not what matters to them—creating an environment that encourages the best ideas to achieve the best result is what matters.

Being the bigger person means putting aside our own ego and prioritising the achievement of shared goals—whether it is developing a new product, winning a major contract or solving an internal problem. When shared goals are the focus, people forget about getting their own way. They focus on the best idea or decision to achieve the goal.

The world's high-performing organisations share a common approach to making the best decisions. They are driven by ideas not hierarchy. When there is disagreement on ideas or a decision, the use their well-defined purpose, values and shared goals to guide the way. In the end, the CEO may be the tiebreaker, but it's a myth that CEOs make all the decisions.

Steve Jobs and Apple Driving the Best Ideas

Many people believe that Steve Jobs made all the decisions at Apple. He led with a strong vision and purpose, but he didn't make all the decisions. In an interview a year before Jobs died, Walt Mossberg uncovered how Jobs led.

Jobs was explaining how he spent most days at Apple. He would meet with functional teams to work on ideas and solve problems on whatever the most pressing goals were.

Mossberg asked Jobs, "Are people willing to tell you that you are wrong?"

Jobs smiled and said, "Yeah, we have wonderful arguments!"

"And do you win?" Mossberg asked.

"Oh no. I wish I did!" Jobs laughed and continued, "You see you can't. If you want to hire great people and have them stay working for you, you have to let them make decisions and be run by ideas, not hierarchy. The best ideas have to win".

Mossberg pressed Jobs, "You must be more than a facilitator who runs meetings. You must contribute your own ideas?"

Jobs replied, "Of course I contribute ideas. Why would I be there if I didn't?". [26]

Jobs was clearly involved and hands-on, but he didn't abuse his position to get his own way. He didn't assume he was the smartest person in the room. He knew and often said he had smart people working at Apple. He became involved to coach, contribute and challenge so that Apple could achieve the best outcomes.

Apple employees who worked with Jobs have publicly confirmed that he was driven by the best idea. They say he would even take the opposite side of an argument to his own, just to encourage debate and ideas from others.

As Jobs once said, "It doesn't make sense to hire smart people and tell them what to do. We hire smart people so they can tell us what to do".[26]

Microsoft Leaving Ego Behind

When Satya Nadella became only the 3rd CEO to lead Microsoft, he said there had been "a lot of ego and hubris" informing Microsoft decisions and that they would fail if they continued down that path. Instead, he took the lead on engaging in two-way dialog with employees, encouraging ideas and input. He explained "Ultimately, the learn-it-all will do better than the know-it-all. And that, I think, is true for CEOs. It's true for companies".[22]

Starbucks Culture of Listening

Starbucks executive Virginia Tenpenny explains Starbucks approach to listening to their people to engage and evolve. She says that the core of their culture and business strategy is "Our 50-year legacy of really listening to people, recognising where there is an issue, where Starbucks has a unique ability to have a positive impact, and ideally bringing other companies along."[14]

"When you are consistently listening to your people and understanding that they need to feel that sense of purpose, to feel that sense of connection to the company. That really guides us in terms of where we can have the greatest impact." [14]

"So much of leadership is about listening. It's about being curious. It's about consistently looking at what are old ways of doing things that maybe no longer serve us ... It's about having the courage to look at things that need to be radically different, (and asking) where do we need to leapfrog into the future?" [14]

Tenpenny supports "creating a learning environment, where we're comfortable to be vulnerable, where we're comfortable to explore and learn and sometimes not get it right, but be committed to continuing on that evolution". [14]

This kind of accelerated engagement, learning and evolution cannot be achieved when leaders see themselves as the smartest person in the room. The final ingredient is making it safe for people to participate.

Tenpenny says, "You create that psychological safety and an environment where people can explore and learn and evolve, and to me that's what I see as core leadership at Starbucks."

Encouraging People to Contribute Ideas

Hands-on leaders need to make it safe for people to contribute ideas. Asking people to speak up doesn't mean they will. They will stay silent until they feel safe and rewarded for contributing. Once they trust it is safe, they will participate.

There are 4 things you can do to make it safe for people to contribute ideas.

- The first is to recognise that speaking up makes some people feel very vulnerable. People know they can be judged and even punished for their opinions. Fix this by making it clear from the executive team to the front-line that everyone is entitled to voice an opinion without fear of prejudice. Said simply: There are no dumb ideas.
- Make it clear that people are welcome to disagree and debate without retaliation, regardless of their status or position.
- Set the expectation that while opinion and debate are welcome, it doesn't mean all ideas will be accepted. The idea that best meets our shared goals is the best idea. The best idea will win.
- Flow this down through your organisation. Performance manage and remove people who don't encourage people to feel safe enough to debate, challenge and contribute ideas and take agreed risks.

The Bottom Line

- High-performing organisations thrive on ideas. Their ideas are better than their peers and competitors.
- Ideas are central to becoming unstuck!
- Great ideas can come from anywhere in the organisation.
- Hands-on leaders leverage the power of the knowledge held in their people.
- Most people want to contribute ideas but need to feel safe and heard when they do. Remove fear of speaking up from your organisation to tap into the best ideas.
- Leaders who act like the smartest person in the room are practicing another form of micromanagement to control rather than lead. Their people hesitate to contribute ideas.
- If you are a leader, it is important to surround yourself with people who will challenge you. The need to listen doesn't go away when you become a CEO or senior leader, it becomes even more important.
- A leader's role isn't to have all the ideas or answers — your role as a leader is to be the motivator and curator of ideas to deliver on the organisation's goals.
- Rather than driving compliance, encourage ideas and debate.
- The best idea wins with hands-on leadership, not the smartest, loudest or most senior person in the room.

3
Get out into the Field

Your next move in being hands-on is to get out into the field.

Getting out into the field is essential for any leader who wants to move their organisation forward and accelerate results. The detail you will learn and the relationships and influence you build are invaluable for steering the organisation toward success.

The well-known leaders mentioned in chapter 1 are constantly connected to their people, operation and customers. They are regularly visible in the operation. They don't limit themselves to quarterly contact via remote townhall meetings. They visit in person and get involved to learn, support and clear the way for their people, all the way to the front-line.

Leaders who have been consultants will find this comes naturally. I was lucky to start my career as a consultant designing technology solutions for customers. This meant spending time in their operations. I walked production lines and warehouses, rode in delivery vans, reviewed product designs and analysed customer interactions with sales and service people. I studied their management controls and the connection (or often disconnection) between the strategic goals and the front line. It was an incredibly satisfying experience that transferred to my own management roles.

When I got into management and then senior leadership roles, it was natural to be curious about my own business. I learned how people worked, how to help them be more successful and how I could ensure my strategy would be executed and get results.

People love it when the boss visits their workplace. They enjoy sharing what they do and their challenges. They don't expect you to know everything or have the answers. They just want to be understood and supported.

The TV series *Undercover Boss* showed surprising benefits and insights when CEOs went undercover and worked with employees and customers in their operations.

They discovered the physical and emotional challenges faced by their employees. They learned that employees often didn't have the tools, training, or processes to do their jobs well. They also learned that customers were frustrated by things that could be easily fixed by empowering employees to make decisions or by simplifying processes. But the biggest surprise was that the CEOs had no idea these things were happening in their organisation.

These undercover bosses also discovered employees with massive amounts of loyalty and dedication. They witnessed communication breakdowns vertically and between departments causing unnecessary friction for employees and customers. They learnt that small details could make a big difference in their operation, and they gained valuable insights into how to improve customer experience and grow revenues while reducing costs.

CEOs and senior executives are not management consultants, but they can take a leaf out of a consultant's book. Professional consultants invest time discovering their client's business, preferences, needs and challenges. They engage at all levels from boardroom to frontline, from strategy to operation. Then they combine that information with their expertise to present strategies that will be accepted and will work for that client. CEOs and senior leaders can do the same by spending more time in the field with their people, products, operation and customers.

Getting into the field will help you find and fix what is making your organisation get stuck. It will connect you to essential information to steer your organisation with confidence. And it will also significantly increase the chances that your strategy will be accepted and executed in operation.

Sadly, it is common today for strategic change initiatives to be disconnected from what will work in operation. I have seen so many examples of organisations where managers and front-line workers are given an initiative that won't work and simply does not make sense in operation.

As well-intentioned as the initiative may be, it creates more problems than it solves. People disengage, lose faith, or simply leave the organisation. And it's the best people who leave first. The initiative only serves to disrupt and distract people from getting results.

Initiatives like this fail because leaders don't have knowledge of the operational detail. Neither do the people advising them. They may have data, but they don't have detail.

Data Without Detail is Dangerous

You can learn more from time in the field than you can looking at the numbers.

Detail is the operational knowledge and experience that validates the data. Ensuring that a strategy will succeed in operation requires both data and detail.

There are many well-intentioned initiatives based on data that have had unintended consequences. For example, Uber's surge pricing looked good on a spreadsheet but initially failed in operation because it lacked the detail to make it practical.

Another failed initiative driven by data without detail to support them was the Australian Government Robodebt scheme. The scheme aimed to recover welfare debt. The algorithm, based on a spreadsheet, was prone to errors and often overestimated income, resulting in thousands of Australians being issued inaccurate debt notices demanding repayment for money they didn't owe.

This caused significant financial hardship and emotional distress for many people.

Decisions based on data without detail are often inaccurate and pose a risk to the outcome of leader's decisions. Consider this example of data without detail:

In the last year, a company lost 70 people from their staff. 88 percent of them received an increase in compensation from their new employer.

Based on the data, it is logical to conclude the organisation is not paying competitive salaries. Your strategy might be to pay more. But would your strategy change if you knew that most people (92%) received a salary increase when they changed jobs? Or if you had the specific details on why they decided to leave? Maybe the new job is closer to home. Maybe they are leaving a "bad boss," or are frustrated by obstacles or other working conditions that can be fixed without paying them more money.

The point is that having the detail can bring greater meaning to the data that is being used to make decisions. Often the most important detail is the human impact—the change required by people to execute the initiative. Understanding this is essential to becoming unstuck and achieving faster execution and results.

Understanding people creates influence and motivation

Embedding strategy, creating alignment and communicating change requires rapport with people.

You can't influence and inspire people to change until they know you understand them and what matters to them. To do that you need to get into the field and spend time understanding people and the operation.

How you can get out into the field

Go out and connect with managers and frontline workers. As a priority, go talk to your people on the frontline. You don't need to have all the answers to their questions, you are not there for that—you are there to listen, learn and understand.

Make it clear you are not there to check up on people. They will assume this until you explain that you are there to listen and learn. And that your goal is to make them more successful which will make the organisation more successful.

Be confidently humble, making it safe for people to share. Ask them to explain how they work. Be on the lookout for challenges, obstacles, lack of tools or stupid processes that disempower them.

Spend time in each location. Go to work with these people in whatever roles they do. Get your hands dirty and be willing to do some of the work where possible. This may take some planning but can be done on subsequent visits.

Talk to users or customers directly. Visit the call center. Answer some calls. Serve customers in the operation. Get involved and engage.

Listen more than you speak to employees. Speak only to encourage them to participate, to thank them for sharing, or to connect the dots in the big picture for them. You don't need to have the answers. You just need to show you understand. This is empathy in business. It builds enormous credibility and influence.

You don't need an entourage or a series of task forces or teams following you around. Just get out there on your own and run with whatever comes up. Everything you learn and observe will be used to move your organisation forward.

If you are in an industry without a large frontline of workers dealing with the operation and customers, get out and use your own products like a customer would. It is amazing what you will learn, and the experience is deeply satisfying.

If you do these things you will experience a profound sense of purpose and empathy which at your level can be directly used to find efficiencies and create innovation that people will get behind and respect you for.

Getting out into the field isn't a one-off event for a hands-on leader. It is a regular event that they enjoy and gain great value from.

Go have fun. Get out into the field.

The Bottom Line

- Hands-on leaders are not stuck behind email all day. They are not stuck in office meetings all day or leadership meetings. They are engaged with their business.
- Getting out into the field ensures that strategies succeed, and opportunities are taken to remove obstacles to allow an organisation to become unstuck!
- Using consultants is not the best way to connect with your people, operation and customers. Do it yourself and your confidence and connection will magnify and so will your success.
- The regular contact, intel and influence that you will gain by getting into the field are invaluable.

4

The Business of Empathy

Hands-on leaders leverage empathy in business. Empathy is a leadership skill that gets business results. Ironically, as people become more successful, they often become less empathetic. It is not intentional or selfish. It is a natural oversight as they become disconnected from the average worker and more focussed on their own needs and continued success.

This makes empathy a rare and competitive differentiator in business—especially when it comes from the top of an organisation.

Empathy is highly visible in many of the world's high-performing organisations. They use empathy to achieve 3 business outcomes:

1. Enhance customer experience to grow revenues.
2. Engage and align their people for performance and innovation.
3. Manage the inevitable crises that damage brands and CEO careers.

Let's get a working definition of empathy and then cover how to use it for those 3 business outcomes.

Empathy is an ability to understand other people. It is understanding their ideas, point of view, situation and most importantly how they feel about it. Empathy is best described as understanding what people think and how they feel—both rationally and emotionally.

Understanding what people think and how they feel is a competitive advantage in business. The customer experience is both rational and emotional. Upset a customer and you lose them. Delight them and they will spend more than is rational. Employee engagement is also both rational and emotional. Confidence in a CEO and brand are both rational and emotional responses.

The American memoirist, poet, and civil rights activist Maya Angelou famously said, "People will forget what you said, people will forget what you did, but people will never forget how you made them feel." This perfectly highlights the importance of understanding how people feel.

Understanding how people feel and what they think is the first part of empathy. It is important you then communicate your understanding and finally take any required action.

It's like when you call your phone or internet company with a problem. You want the agent to quickly understand your situation and its importance and then to take action to fix the issue to your satisfaction.

Empathy has three important parts:

1. **Understand** other people—specifically being able to understand their situation, what they think about it, how they feel about it and what they need.
2. **Communicate** your understanding. Empathy is useless if people don't know that you understand.
3. **Take action** to give people what they need.

Here's the formula for Empathy:

Empathy = Understand + Communicate + Act

Applying Empathy in Business

Let's apply empathy to the three business outcomes of high-performing organisations: Enhance customer experience; Align and engage people; and Manage Crises that damage brands and CEO careers.

1. Enhancing customer experience.

Empathy in customer experience can be proactive or reactive. Reactive empathy is where a product or service has failed to meet expectations. It is about quickly understanding, communicating and acting promptly to fix the issue and enhance how the customer feels. This kind of empathy repairs trust and loyalty and protects revenue and reputations.

Proactive empathy in customer experience involves understanding customer needs, designing products, processes or technology to meet those needs and then communicating and offering it to customers. The customer's experience of empathy is all contained in the final product and how they think and feel is the measure of success.

> *Proactive empathy in action*
> *A product example of proactive empathy is OXO*
> *'Good Grips' kitchen tools. They are designed to be*
> *comfortable and easy to use for people with limited*
> *hand strength. The design team conducted research*
> *on people with arthritis and other disabilities to*
> *identify common pain points in kitchen tools. The*
> *OXO Good Grips tools have thick, easy-to-grip*
> *handles and non-slip surfaces that make them easier*
> *to use for everyone.*

Products designed with empathy are lucrative. They create loyal customers who spend more for the enhanced experience. Empathy can create significant competitive advantage in customer experience. Improvements in customer-facing technology, business processes (such as product returns) and customer call centres are ripe opportunities for empathy in action.

2. Engaging and aligning people in your organisation.

Empathy is like a backstage pass at a rock concert

when trying to connect with and align with people. I recently coached a chairman who was having trouble managing a board member who was bullying the new CEO over recent hits to profitability. The CEO was getting frustrated because he had briefly explained the profit issue was under control, but the board member wouldn't let it go. The CEO needed to gain approvals for an important initiative, but the board member wanted detail after detail about the profit situation. The chairman was at a loss as to how to manage the dynamic between the board member and CEO.

I suggested empathy. The board member was anxious and this needed to be acknowledged to allow him to move on. He needed to hear that the CEO understood and appreciated his concerns. He then needed to see a clear action plan to a level that made him comfortable.

At the next board meeting, the CEO started using empathy (understand + communicate + act) to address the board member's concerns and the meeting went much smoother. The dynamic between the board member and CEO also improved.

Empathy can be used to create alignment across teams. Many teams have conflicting goals, redundant processes, approval bottlenecks and other needs. Expressing an understanding of and taking action to remove their problems is a powerful use of empathy that can engage and align teams.

Empathy is a communication skill that can melt resistance to new initiatives. It can do this by calling out your understanding of people's concerns, needs and how you have designed the initiative to fit with those concerns and needs.

For example, say you are investing in a new hand-held technology that replaces desktop admin work for delivery reps. Resistance to a change that impacts someone's daily work tasks is normal. But if you show you understand their current work challenges, then explain how the new tech will reduce admin time at the end of the day, allowing them to leave early, they will respect you and give it a go. You may need to choose an influencer to try it, but empathy is the key here.

The upfront effort you put into using empathy will be far less than the effort to fight resistance by having to push people every day to complete a project when they are resisting change. A project like this will propel itself if people feel understood and that their needs are met.

3. Managing crises that damage brands and CEO careers.

Empathy can save brands and careers when used with skill. When the original iPhone was launched, Steve Jobs gave a masterclass in empathy to recover from a mistake Apple made that could have damaged the uptake of the first iPhone. It was a critical point in Apple's success and growth.

Apple dropped the price of its new iPhone 2 months after launch. The decision backfired, enraging early adopters who paid full price. Disappointment replaced delight, causing a PR nightmare.

Jobs' response was consistent with the empathy formula of: **Understand + Communicate + Act**

Understand

Jobs took the time to read hundreds of emails from customers complaining. After taking time to understand what customers thought and felt, he gave us a masterclass in communicating empathy in a business.

Communicate

Jobs started by acknowledging that he had read the emails and understood people were "upset about Apple dropping the price of the iPhone by $200 two months after it went on sale."

He then expertly framed the situation, so everyone was looking at it through the same lens. He explained that dropping the price benefitted Apple and every iPhone user by getting more customers into the iPhone "tent". He explained that technology by nature is always changing, improving and prices dropping. If you wait for the price cut or new model you will never buy any technology.

All these statements were true, but he didn't use any of this as an excuse—that would have ruined any attempt at empathy—he simply set reasonable expectations before expressing empathy and taking action to make it right.

He communicated empathy saying given the price drop is appropriate and is to be expected, "we need to do a better job taking care of our early iPhone customers as we aggressively go after new ones with a lower price. Our early customers trusted us, and we must live up to that trust with our actions in moments like these".[23]

Act

Jobs then offered early customers a $100 credit. This was largely well-received because of the lens he put on it at the start. He had understood and managed what people thought and how they felt.

He finished with a perfect apology that put more weight to it all. He said "We want to do the right thing for our valued iPhone customers. We apologise for disappointing some of you, and we are doing our best to live up to your high expectations of Apple".

It was a balanced, relevant and near perfect use of empathy in business to manage a crisis. Early adopters always pay more than those who wait, but two months was a very short time for a price drop, so he acknowledged how they felt and then fixed it. And he did it quickly.

The timing of empathy is essential in a crisis. Within 24 hours of dropping the price, Apple recognised it had made a mistake, managed expectations, showed they understood, issued an apology and took action to make it right in a way that people valued.

When empathy is not used skilfully to resolve crises

The negative consequences of not using empathy as skilfully as Steve Jobs can be greatly damaging to brands and their leaders.

While writing this book, Optus, Australia's second largest broadband and mobile phone carrier, had a national network outage. It ended with the CEO resigning. The outage lasted approximately 14 hours. A big deal? Sure. But one that the CEO should resign over? Absolutely not.

The need to recover from this crisis had to be managed carefully and quickly because Optus had experienced a cyber-attack the previous year that left concerns and trust issues with both consumers and regulators.

Unfortunately, the response from Optus was slow and unclear at times. It didn't meet expectations and damaged confidence in the brand and the CEO. This loss of confidence unnecessarily cost the CEO her job.

The events in summary were:
1. Approximately 30% of Australian's woke up to no internet, no mobile phones and no emergency numbers for ambulance, police and fire.
2. The CEO did not appear publicly for around 6 hours.
3. The federal government criticised the CEO's lack of communication.
4. Customers and small businesses demanded compensation.

5. Anger and frustration boiled over as people wanted answers.

6. The CEO eventually said the problem was too technical to explain.

7. Most services were restored by the end of the day.

8. The CEO offered people 200gb of free data and an apology.

9. A senate inquiry said Optus failed to show empathy for its customers.

Could better use of empathy have helped Optus?

The approach Steve Jobs took might have saved the CEO of Optus. It could have gone something like this:

1. A quick response to start communication.

Rather than let fear and anger grow, the CEO could have communicated sooner to reassure people. Optus has huge resources and expertise that they no doubt deployed. Telling the public something like: "We are aware of the problem and the urgent need to get services restored for everyone. At this early stage we don't know the cause, but we have over 300 engineers in 150 locations working hard to restore services as soon as possible. It is common for outages to take a few hours to fix. We understand how troubling this is and will report back as soon as we have more information." This would have shown empathy for the urgency of the situation.

2. A reframe before offering a solution.

When it came time to report the solution and discuss compensation, the CEO might have used Jobs' framing of his industry to the upset customers. I'm not an expert in Telecommunication regulations, but the Optus CEO could have explained that utilities (power, water, internet) will always experience outages—for example electricity companies have blackouts that can last days. When this happens, electricity companies don't issue compensation, insurance companies do that. However we want to do the right thing...

3. A communication of sincere understanding.

Similar to Jobs, Optus could have said something like, "Our customers trust us with their connection to work, customers, family and emergency services. While we cannot behave like an insurance company, we want to do the right thing for our customers.."

4. Action.

Rather than offer customers 200gb of free data which was worthless to most of them, perhaps a refund or credit of 24 hours (more than the 14 hour outage) would have been seen as reasonable in the context of not being an insurance company for utility failures.

5. Further underlining their commitment

A proactive statement recognising the importance of connectivity for consumers and businesses, followed with a firm commitment to work with regulators and other providers about lessons learned.

The response example above could have been polished by industry experts, but the formula is the key to managing this and other crises that threaten the brand, the CEO and the organisation.

Empathy is not about avoiding conflict. It is about being willing to jump in even when it is uncomfortable. Empathy requires commitment. You need to do the work to understand people's situations, what they think and how they feel, then determine what you can do to give them what they need.

Remember to use empathy

Empathy is a skill that can be learned and used with skill. But what is more important is to remember to use it in the first place. There are times when we need to be aware of our inclination not to use empathy.

Empathy is the act of focussing on other people's needs. When we are focussed on our own needs, we lose empathy. A common cause of lost empathy is when we feel threatened or defensive. Or when we feel superior to others. At these times, our ego is engaged and we are focussed on ourselves.

There is a backstory to the way Steve Jobs' handled complaints about the iPhone price drop. His original reaction, behind closed doors, was defensive, offended and possibly superior. The iPhone was a world-wide success when it launched. Orders flooded in. Share prices of all other phone makers dropped instantly. The world press agreed that Apple had reinvented the phone. Jobs was on a high. How could people be complaining? His ego was first to respond, but hours later, he put his ego aside and focussed his masterful skill in using empathy to meet his customer's needs. This is also another demonstration of Apple's focus on customer experience that resulted in extraordinary growth and profits.

A Gentle Warning

Empathy is so powerful it can be enticing to fake it. But empathy cannot be faked. Organisations and people who use hollow words that are later found to be insincere and hypocritical often damage their credibility and lose all influence over others. Greenwashing and other insincere expressions of empathy are quickly revealed as being manipulative. They result is the opposite of genuine empathy— broken trust, lost loyalty, damaged reputations and brands. Be sincere. Be real. The results are worth the effort.

One last thing...

Apart from the positive business outcomes achieved with empathy, there is another positive personal outcome: It feels great! When you use empathy, you feel great. When you receive empathy, you feel great. People and organisations that use empathy are loved and respected by those they serve.

The Bottom Line

- If you are not practicing empathy as a leader, your time is running out.
- If your organisation's people, products and services are not using empathy you're slipping behind and opening the door for competitors, opposition parties in government, or new leaders to take your position.
- Without empathy you are becoming stuck.
- Great leaders today are using empathy in their organisation with amazing results.
- Empathy is your competitive advantage.
- There is a formula, structure and process to using empathy in business.
- Anyone can learn and apply empathy in business for business results.

Factor #2
Purpose-Led Culture

The second factor leveraged by high-performing organisations is a purpose-led culture.

A purpose-led culture is an organisation's ability to create commitment and support for the reason it exists beyond making money. At its best, a purpose-led culture will gain support from employees, customers, shareholders and other stakeholders.

It is impossible to lead a company to perform at its full potential without a clear purpose and a culture designed to support that purpose.

Purpose makes everything simpler, easier and faster. It creates incredible levels of performance that can be used to achieve exceptional results.

In this section we dive into the "why", "what" and "how" of purpose so you can leverage your organisation's purpose to achieve exceptional results.

5
The Purpose of Purpose

Purpose is found at the heart of many of the world's high-performing organisations. It unites and motivates their people to achieve exceptional results. Many successful startups achieve rapid results and success because of the internal and external commitment to their purpose. As organisations grow, they can lose the effect of their purpose, but it doesn't have to be that way at all. Purpose can increase performance and results regardless of how established an organisation is.

Take LEGO, a 90+ year old organisation. You would be forgiven for thinking LEGO had been left behind by new technology toys. Instead, it continues to be the much loved and largest toy maker in the world. Their simple yet effective purpose is: "To inspire and develop children through play". This is all about the power of play and creativity in child development. Their purpose works because it is consistent with their strategy and their customers' and employees' values. LEGO is the most valuable toy brand in the world for the tenth consecutive year.

Their financial, customer and employee scores are industry leading.

SpaceX, a much younger organisation, has transformed the aerospace industry in ways that the larger, more established players could not. Their purpose has attracted some of the brightest minds in engineering, while motivating them to achieve extraordinary results. Their people, despite numerous setbacks, have achieved groundbreaking advancements in space travel that all other aerospace players are now following. The impact of their purpose is undeniably linked with their ability to overcome obstacles to achieve remarkable results.

SpaceX was founded on the purpose "to revolutionize space technology, with the ultimate goal of enabling people to live on other planets". This purpose is only part of what inspires SpaceX employees.

Their purpose is strongly supported by ambitious goals like building "reusable launch vehicles that will be the most powerful ever built, capable of carrying humans to Mars and other destinations in the solar system", and their willingness to push the boundaries of what is possible, to take risks and to learn from (not be punished by) failures. This is all embodied in SpaceX's Purpose. It is no wonder SpaceX has high-performing people who achieve such remarkable results.

Any organisation can do this. Don't be fooled into thinking SpaceX's purpose is only effective because it is world-changing. Their purpose is effective because people are given a worthy cause that they believe in,

PLUS a challenge to improve the status quo, PLUS
the freedom to try to do it. This formula could be used
in any industry such as healthcare, hospitality, toys or
automotive—and you know what, it already is being
used in many industries by the world's high-
performing organisations like LEGO and others
mentioned in this book.

The Benefits of an Effective Purpose

There are several benefits that come from an effective
purpose.

Benefit #1 Purpose-led organisations outperform others.

The studies and the data are compelling: Purpose-led
organisations are 2.5 times more effective at
innovation and transformation. They have 40%
higher employee retention and engagement. They
attract customers who are loyal, pay more for their
products and refer them to other customers. Purpose-
led organisations also consistently outperform the
stock market.[5]

Several studies correlate purpose with performance,
higher profit, brand-value and growth. One study of
500,000 employees across 500 companies found a
measurable link between purpose and performance.[10]

Benefit #2 Purpose is a source of great leadership power.

The ability to articulate a meaningful purpose generates buy-in and support from employees, customers, investors and other stakeholders such as the media, analysts and voters.

Think about some of the most influential leaders in history. Martin Luther King Jr changed the hearts and minds of millions world-wide when he talked about equality regardless of a person's race. JFK united a nation to achieve one of the greatest feats in human history—"landing a man on the moon and returning him safely to the earth".

In 1997, Steve Jobs' returned to Apple to find the company in financial ruin. He made one observation: Apple had betrayed its core purpose. He spent 6 weeks thinking deeply about and restating Apple's core purpose. It inspired investors, analysts and employees to support the radical changes needed to save Apple from bankruptcy, and to eventually become the largest company on the planet then and even today being in the top 3 largest companies.

That same year, Jeff Bezos took Amazon public with a purpose so well-articulated and constantly reinforced that Amazon eventually became the largest online retailer.

As a successful, purpose led leader, you don't need to be charismatic or extroverted and you don't need to change the world or land someone on the moon. Anyone can articulate a purpose. It just has to be real and to resonate with people.

Benefit #3 Purpose makes decisions easier

Purpose gives leaders a compass to not only avoid difficult situations but also to navigate them when they happen. Purpose clarifies what is important and what the organisation stands for. When tough times call for tough decisions, purpose provides the foundation on which to make those decisions.

Benefit # 4 Purpose Dissolves Resistance to Change

Purpose is essential to the success of change initiatives. Change is constant today, yet it is still being done the old way, pushed from the top down without engaging people on why or tapping into their sense of purpose. Purpose-led change provides relevance and meaning to people at all levels. People will choose change when it aligns with an effective and agreed purpose.

Benefit #5 Purpose Creates Collaboration

People work better together in purpose-led organisations. Purpose unites people with a shared identity and a wider view of their role and how it relates to the organisation's purpose. When an organisation's purpose is understood, departments will remove barriers and collaborate around this common purpose and shared goals. An integrated purpose leads to integrated departments driven to contribute to and fulfil that purpose.

Benefit #6 Purpose Provides Focus

Finally, a meaningful purpose will refocus how you do business. Purpose-driven organisations shift from having an internal company-focus to an external customer-focus. The difference is significant.

When organisations get lost in their own numbers and lose focus on their customers, they eventually lose their way. A purpose with an external customer focus is a promise to add value for people other than ourselves.

When your employees believe in and commit to keeping that promise, they become aligned, inspired and accountable for achieving extraordinary things.

However, you must avoid internal company-focused purpose statements that are about being the best, the biggest, number one in the industry, growing market share etc. These kinds of purpose statements are not inspirational or meaningful to most people inside your organisation. Customer-focused purpose statements are far more inspiring, and the results of high-performing organisations that use them speak for themselves.

Virgin's purpose statement at the start of the 21st century was "We believe in making a difference. In our customers' eyes, Virgin stands for value for money, quality, innovation, fun and a sense of competitive challenge. We deliver a quality service by empowering our employees and we facilitate and monitor customer feedback to continually improve the customer's experience through innovation."

What is the Purpose of Purpose?

An effective purpose will unite and inspire people to act. It will attract people to join your organisation and work together to achieve exceptional results. Customers, investors and other stakeholders will also be drawn to support your organisation and its purpose.

The Bottom Line

- Purpose powers performance.
- Purpose is critical for engaged employees, successful change, effective collaboration and for becoming unstuck to achieve better results faster.
- Purpose-led organisations outperform others in almost every measure: speed of execution, innovation, employee engagement, customer loyalty, profit, growth and reputation.
- The effects that purpose-led organisations achieve with purpose are possible for any organisation.
- If your organisation isn't getting the results you'd like, if it's moving slower than you'd like, or if it's going through a business transformation, there's a strong case for revisiting purpose to accelerate results.

6
What Purpose is and How it Works

Today, many organisations are not asking "if" they can leverage purpose for exceptional results, they are asking "how" they can do this.

Despite the popularity of organisational purpose, there is confusion around exactly what purpose is and how it works. Studies show that for purpose to contribute to performance, it must go beyond superficial statements that people don't connect with or are unable to enact in their daily work.

What Purpose Is

Purpose is the foundation that supports vision and mission. Vision is an organisation's "where" we want to be in the future. Mission is an organisation's "what and how" we will get there. Purpose is an organisation's "why". It answers the question of why we exist and who we serve.

Purpose is the reason an organisation exists. It is the fundamental beliefs and values that drive everything the organisation does. It is the impact the organisation has on other people beyond making money.

How Purpose Works

Everyone needs a purpose in life to be fulfilled. Work fills so much of our lives that we naturally seek purpose at work. Without purpose we feel unfulfilled, obstacles appear larger and our energy feels lower. With purpose we perform better, we feel better, we overcome obstacles and are more successful in what we do. There is nothing else like it for sustained drive, fulfilment and performance.

On a personal level, our purpose is the meaning that we find in our work, beyond money that drives us to do that work, even when it is challenging. Meaning usually comes from doing something we believe in and care about that contributes to something bigger than us. In organisations this is creating value for those we serve such as customers.

We create value by solving a problem or improving a situation using our expertise and focus. When we have a meaningful purpose, it evokes emotions of care and enthusiasm. We try harder because we care.

What do you put extra effort into? I'll bet it is things you care about and find meaningful.

Why Does This Work?

As humans we have 2 types of motivators that drive us to achieve goals: internal and external motivators. External motivators come from outside the individual. They are rewards and punishments. Money is an external motivator.

Internal motivators come from within an individual. They are meaning and fulfilment from contributing to something larger that aligns with our values. Purpose is an internal motivator.

High-performing organisations recognise that people need both external and internal motivators. They set targets with external rewards like money and time-off and combine these with the internal motivator of a meaningful purpose that aligns with people's values. The fulfilment that comes from contributing to something bigger, that makes an impact on others and is a strong motivator beyond mere goals and metrics.

In contrast, organisations without a meaningful purpose lead with financial and operational goals, timelines and aspirational targets. These are fine but alone don't inspire people to challenge their own limits and do their absolute best work.

"They don't pay me enough to do this job" is often heard when purpose is lacking. When purpose is present, you'll see people going above and beyond. For instance, emergency service men and women rush into danger not because they are being paid, but because they are driven by purpose. This behaviour isn't limited to firefighters and healthcare professionals. There are many corporate organisations with people driven to achieve the organisation's purpose, such as those mentioned earlier—LEGO, SpaceX, Marriott, Apple and many others.

The final ingredient in making purpose work is enabling people to act. There is no use having a motivating purpose that people can't contribute to in their daily work.

People need the ability and authority to make decisions or take action when required to fulfil the purpose. There are many ways to do this such as granting employees that ability to make discretionary decisions to solve customer problems or flexibility to do their work within guidelines. The best way to find the right enablers is in discussions with your people once the purpose is defined and being put into operation.

The Bottom Line

- Purpose is the reason an organisation exists, beyond making money. It is the impact the people and the organisation have on other people. Purpose at work is contributing to something we value that is bigger than ourselves.
- People have external motivators (rewards and punishments) and internal motivators like purpose that provides meaning, fulfilment and personal achievement that matters to them.
- Purpose will motivate people to do their best work, try harder and get out of their comfort zones to achieve the fulfilment that comes from achieving a meaningful purpose.
- Purpose works when it is meaningful and people have the ability and authority to act on achieving the purpose in their day-to-day work.
- Purpose is essential to becoming unstuck!

7

Creating Your Organisation's Purpose

PwC's Global CEO Survey found that less than half (41%) of CEOs believe their employees are aligned with corporate goals and values. This suggests employees are disconnected from the purpose of their work.

Studies also reveal that while most organisations believe purpose is important, they find it difficult to articulate and integrate purpose to drive performance. Attempts to do this often only scratch the surface. They are not reflected in operation and are not memorable or inspiring to employees and customers. They are often seen as superficial marketing catchphrases that nobody takes seriously.

The good news is that many of the world's high-performing organisations have successfully created and implemented their purpose. They also see a direct link between their purpose and their performance. The difference is in how they approach purpose.

High-performing organisations have thought deeply about their purpose and values. Their purpose is often simple and meaningful in a way that everyone can connect with. It is a true reflection of what their organisation does, what it stands for and it comes from an authentic place.

Founder CEOs have the edge on everyone else when it comes to implementing a purpose that drives results. Jeff Bezos, Mark Zuckerberg, Steve Jobs, Marc Benioff, Bill Gates, Elon Musk, Warren Buffett, Walt Disney and many others were known for their clear purpose. Whether you like these leaders or not, the fact is this: these leaders achieved exceptional results with their purpose.

The reason their purpose had such impact was their emotional and logical connection to it, and their ability to connect their people with it. Their purpose is personal. They live and breathe their purpose. Every day.

The other reason for the success of their purpose is the approach they take to creating and implementing a purpose. Founders don't approach purpose as a copywriting exercise. Their purpose comes from deep reflection. They don't develop it in isolation. They involve leaders, employees and customers.

When it is finally articulated into words, they don't see it as finished. That's just the beginning for them. They infuse their purpose into strategy, operations and culture with constant communication, actions and daily decisions that are consistent with their purpose.

High-performing organisations measure and reinforce their purpose as an ongoing process. If you listen to any of their founders talk, you will hear elements of their purpose echoed in media interviews, comments to staff and stories about their industry and organisation. They live and breathe their purpose every day.

Creating Your Organisation's Purpose

You may not be a founder, but you can adopt a founder's mindset by making it personal, emotional and logical for yourself and everyone else involved. To do that your purpose needs to be true to your organisation, its expertise and the impact it has (and can have) for those it serves.

Leaders often ask what a purpose should focus on and what it should contain. Should purpose be cultural—the reason and values behind what we do? Should it be for a social, economic or human cause—the impact we have on others? Or should it be our expertise—the products and services we provide?

The answer is yes to all three. A purpose is comprised of the reason and values behind why we do what we do, the people we impact and the expertise we bring.

Having a purpose doesn't mean you have to save people's lives, solve global warming or end world hunger. Purpose must align with your organisation's expertise and values in a way that solves your customers' problems or improves their lives.

Articulate, Integrate and Measure

The approach outlined here is something you can use in your own organisation. I have used it myself for my own teams and for my clients.

There are three stages to implementing your purpose. First, you must articulate your organisation's purpose, then integrate it in the organisation and finally measure its success.

- ARTICULATE
- INTEGRATE
- MEASURE

STAGE 1: ARTICULATE

Articulating your organisation's purpose is a process of uncovering it and then putting it into words.

If you have customers, your organisation already has a purpose. And there are people working in your organisation who know it and believe in it.

The place to start is by engaging in conversations with your people and then with your customers. These conversations need to be framed in the context of the current situation and reason for creating or revisiting purpose, which will vary. For example, you may be a new leader or have a new leadership team, or the organisation might be at a point of growth, change or reinvention. These are all great opportunities and reasons to revisit purpose and have these conversations.

Once the context is clear, the goal of the conversations is to uncover the value you create, the problems you solve for customers, the expertise you bring and the passion your people have for it.

This kind of leadership requires a hands-on approach. It requires direct involvement with people, encouraging and listening to their ideas. It requires empathy to understand and verbally acknowledge what they think and how they feel. The result is an ability to craft a purpose that resonates with people immediately. That is a purpose that can then be put into action.

It is common for leaders who want to connect people, purpose and results to become hands on. New Starbucks CEO Laxman Narasimhan told employees that he'll work a half day every month at one of the cafes. He even went through 40 hours of barista training. He said he wanted to stay close to employees, customers and the culture, no doubt to understand the existing purpose so he can better articulate and integrate this into his strategy and operations to drive results.

What if you're running an organisation that requires specialised skills like an airline or a hospital? You can't go fly a plane or operate on a patient, but you can spend time in the cockpit, or in the hospital theatre, and in operations connecting with people, ideas and knowledge.

Your role as a leader is to curate ideas, not come up with all of them. Some of your people will give you great ideas, others will have ideas that are misguided or impractical, but all are worth listening to so you can understand your people and uncover the great ideas.

When listening to your people you are not there to make decisions or agree. Just listen. When you eventually articulate the purpose, you may also need to acknowledge the ideas that didn't make it and why in the context of the purpose. Doing that will bring those people along rather than leave them behind.

To achieve this as a CEO or senior leader you are going to have to walk the halls, spend time talking with the front-line workers and their managers. This becomes easy when you create an environment where people trust you and what you are trying to achieve. Creating trust can be as simple as explaining why you want to know, sharing your own thoughts to get the conversation started, and showing you care. Once you share, they will share. But remember, it's not all about your ideas. You are there to listen and encourage them to share.

When you create an environment where people are convinced your intention is to honestly reinvigorate your organisation's purpose they will open up.

Another benefit of getting involved and connecting with people at all levels is that you will find the people you need to power your purpose—the influencers and the ones who care and believe in the purpose. They will reveal themselves with their ideas and their passion.

You've got this. Remember, this isn't a feel-good exercise. It is a highly empowering study that puts essential information in your hands as a leader.

Let's get started on Stage 1 Articulate.

How to Articulate a purpose

There are three parts to articulating a purpose – the personal, the commercial and the meaningful.

Before you begin you need to prepare by framing up where you are coming from. You might kick off the conversation with something along these lines:

> "At XYZ Co, we are entering a [Challenging or Exciting or New] period in our history. Over the next few years, we have the opportunity to (or need to or will face) [INSERT SITUATION].
>
> I am having conversations with people to understand what we stand for and what our purpose really is. By purpose, I mean the value we add and the problems we solve for customers with our expertise and resources".

Next, consider the three parts below to begin uncovering and articulating a purpose that will unite and inspire people to act.

Part 1: PERSONAL

Purpose is personal. It is the stuff we care about, are proud of and believe in. It is both the emotional and logical stuff. An effective purpose is held in the heads and hearts of your leaders, employees and customers.

To connect with this, you need to be able to understand and connect to their point of view, knowledge and wisdom. Keep products out for now and focus on people. This is the personal, pride-based stuff.

Ask your people questions like these:
Who are we and what do we stand for?

Here's an example I wrote:

> *At Qantas—We are Australia's Premier Airline.*
> *Written on the side of every one of our planes are the*
> *words "The Spirit of Australia". We stand for*
> *Mateship—The Australian spirit of equality, loyalty*
> *and friendship. We live this every day in the way we*
> *care for each other and our customers to create the*
> *safest, most satisfying travel experience possible.*

Ask yourself and your people from leaders to front-liners, questions like:

"What do we really care about in our business?"
"What are we passionate about?"
"Where do you think we add value to our customers?"
"What do we do for customers that makes us proud?"
"How do these things make a difference in their lives?"
"What are we really good at as an organisation?"
"Which of these makes you look forward to coming to work?"
"What other problems can and should we be solving for our customers?"

Turbocharge Your Purpose

This next one is where the magic happens. My mentor, friend and best-selling author of nearly 40 books, Bill O'Hanlon, helped me find my passion and purpose many years ago. He did it by extending the idea of "following your bliss", to "following your bliss and your piss" or in other words: the things that you love and the things that piss you off.

Ask yourself and your people, "If you were a customer what drives you nuts about us, our industry, products or customer experience?"

And then, "What do you love about our industry, products and services?"

Keep it Constructive

You can use "bliss" and "piss" questions anyway you want to uncover the passion people have and their ideas. If you are concerned it will turn into a BMW (Bitching, Moaning and Whining) conversation, simply frame it up first with "We don't want to spiral into negativity, but we do need to tap into what drives us. Let's on what we stand for and keep it constructive."

Other ways to uncover the good and the bad are to ask your people, especially your front-liners, "How are we doing? What are we doing badly? How could we improve on the value and experience we offer our customers?

The answers you get should be charged with emotion and passion. You'll need to sort through the personal grudges and agendas to get to the genuine passion and care that your top people have for your customers, the industry and their work.

The final conversation is with a selection of customers. The goal is to get into the customer's shoes and ask questions like, "What frustrates the hell out of you? What do you wish was faster, easier, simpler, more reliable? What do you love about the product, industry, or service? What do you want more of? What do you want less of? What should we keep doing?"

At the end of these conversations, you will have a good set of ideas. The next step is to test it for commercial viability.

Part 2: COMMERCIAL

For a purpose to be viable it must be commercial. Specifically, can you make a profit? Or if not-for-profit, is it financially viable for you within your budget constraints. If you are solving problems and adding value using your expertise with people who care deeply about "why", then it should be financially viable. If not, then it isn't right for your organisation.

What do customers buy or get from us now? And how is the customer currently underserved, confused, frustrated or dissatisfied?

Some leadership teams would say they already know this, but if they are honest with themselves, they are not as close to the customer as they would like to be. Regardless, this is something that needs to be validated. Getting into the customer's shoes is not a time for assumptions. This is where the business skill of empathy and the practice of hands-on leadership pay dividends.

The first place to gain this insight is from your front-line, customer-facing people. The stories and real experiences you gain here will bring context and meaning to the data.

The next place to gain this information is directly from customers. Any leader can have a conversation directly with customers. There are many ways to do this in a safe and open way. The final way is to collect data from social media, call centers and other platforms.

What do your customers think? And how do they feel? How they feel is more important than what they think. It is important how your organisation, its people, products and services make customers feel. If you take a customer from being frustrated, anxious or annoyed to being satisfied, confident and comfortable then you have a loyal customer, and maybe even a brand champion.

Ask yourself: What value can we create for our customer by solving a problem or improving a situation?

This value may be in things you already do, or it may be represented in the refocus or innovation you are looking for.

Start first with problems and then move to products. In Factor #3 Customer Centricity, we discuss starting with the customer experience and working back to our products in more detail. For now, what problems do we or can we solve?

Ask yourself: How can we help our customers add value to their own customers?

This is where we turn our focus to our expertise and core business: what problems we solve and the outstanding value we and our products offer.

But don't stop there. Ask yourself the following questions:

- Do we have the expertise to deliver?
- What are our competitors doing?
- How can we differentiate ourselves?
- Can we compete and win in (part or all) the problem we solve?

We use these questions to improve how we create value for our customers. The focus is on us and our customer. Don't be overly focused on competitors.

- Can we improve the customer experience?
- What part of the solution or market can we serve successfully?

At the end of this step, you are ready to begin turning these ideas into words. You can start drafting your purpose yourself. The final step is to ensure it is meaningful. This involves articulating your purpose in a way that is authentic, simple and specific.

Part 3: MEANINGFUL

To be meaningful, a purpose statement must be something we aspire to. It needs to be ambitious yet achievable. It must be authentic not superficial. It should be specific and simple, not vague or complicated. And it needs to be something you would be proud to say to your family and friends about what your organisation stands for.

Ambitiously Achievable vs Assumed

An ambitiously achievable purpose statement does three things:

- It is easily understood
- Solves a problem or adds value for others
- Immediately resonates with people in an emotional way

You'll see immediate head nodding, smile inducing, "I want that" reactions.

Starbucks purpose is "To inspire and nurture the human spirit—one person, one cup, one neighbourhood at a time". This has been shown to be the unifying principle that Starbucks employees connect with that consistently shows up in their well-documented business and social initiatives.

For example, Tesla's original purpose statement was "To accelerate the advent of sustainable transport by bringing compelling mass-market electric cars to market as soon as possible." It worked and they delivered ahead of the industry.

Apple's combined statement is "to bring the best user experience to customers through innovative hardware, software, and services....to make the best products on earth and to leave the world better than we found it."

The Apple purpose statement is a good study in being ambitiously achievable vs assumed. If they had just said "To bring the best experience to our customers" that would be assumed. We all assume organisations are going to bring the best experience for us as customers.

Apple make it meaningful and ambitiously achievable by adding the additional parts about innovative products and services and best products and leaving the world better that they found it.

Some purpose statements say pretty much what the organisation already does which most people assume, so they are not very inspirational. The reaction is "So what?" unless is has more heart and meaning.

Other purpose statements say things like, "create value for our customers" or "Provide the highest level of service." Again, these are assumed and expected by customers and employees and just seem like hollow words.

Some corporate purpose statements are marketing catchphrases. They don't mean much in practice and employees can't link their day-to-day activities to contribute to the purpose, but they look and sound slick. And that brings us to authentic vs superficial purpose statements.

Authentic vs Superficial: The Pub Test

In Australia we are quick to call B.S. on people (especially in power) who are fake or self-serving. We often talk about things not passing 'the pub test'. The pub test is a measure of public opinion and acceptance of an idea or subject. The pub test also involves a more relaxed atmosphere where people will be truthful and more inclined to be emotional. A purpose statement needs to pass the test in this honest and open environment. Try these questions to test how it would pass:

Would you feel comfortable telling your friends at the pub over a beer what your company purpose was - using the exact words it is written in?

Would they nod their heads and agree it was of value and needed by people?

Would they call B.S. on its practicality, real-world value, or any of the corporate-speak words?

Specific and Simple vs Vague and Complicated

Overly wordy, jargon-heavy or big-word purpose statements are hard to get inspired by or to put into action.

A vague purpose that you can't immediately action is a hollow purpose. For example, a purpose such as "To provide superior service to targeted customers" is vague. Superior service could mean 5 different things to 5 different people. Instead, it must be specific in the difference it makes and the problem it solves.

A purpose that is too general or has too many goals and aspirations won't inspire anyone.

A great example of a specific and simple purpose statement is In-N-Out Burger's:

> "Providing the freshest, highest quality foods and services for a profit, and a spotless, sparkling environment whereby the customer is our most important asset."

This purpose statement is specific and simple but also meaningful, actionable and personal.

Whenever I am in the US in a city with an In-N-Out Burger store I love to visit to watch the spark in the eyes of every employee who works there. Their purpose statement is authentic and has a positive impact on both their customers and employees.

STAGE 2: INTEGRATE

After uncovering the meaning and words to articulate your purpose, the next stage is to integrate it into your strategy, operations and culture. Connecting people to your purpose is one of the most important jobs of a hands-on leader.

Leaders are responsible for not only articulating a purpose but also ensuring their own and other's communications, decisions and actions are consistent with and demonstrate the purpose on an ongoing basis.

Integrating a purpose requires alignment, communication and demonstration.

Alignment

Strategy, decisions and actions need to align with your purpose for it to be effective. Purpose should direct and inform daily decisions and actions. Many organisations with an effective purpose also set goals or incentives and reward people for behaviours and accomplishments that are consistent with their purpose.

Next, it is essential to empower your people to demonstrate the purpose with their actions. People can't integrate purpose into their work if they don't have the ability to act. Review processes and procedures to ensure people can make decisions in their daily work that align with the organisation's purpose and core values. Giving people some discretionary power to enact the purpose goes a long way.

For example, flight attendants are empowered to make decisions to delight customers or repair poor experiences, like giving impromptu upgrades, free meals or drinks. When your people have some discretionary power, they feel more committed and more accountable to the purpose.

Conversely, there is no point in having a purpose statement that people cannot live up to because they don't have the power to. An example is a call center. Call centers are regularly criticised—but the interesting thing is that complaints come from both frustrated customers and frustrated call center employees. They both have the same complaints: lack of knowledge and decision-making power to help customers, and high call volumes that frustrate customers and overwhelm agents.

Creating alignment to your purpose statement means taking the time to ensure employees are empowered to live up to the purpose statement.

Continual Communication of your Purpose!

Communication is essential to ensure your purpose is integrated and acted on. Communication is often underdone. Hands-off leaders under-communicate. Purpose is a form of direction-setting, decision-making and accountability. It is not possible to over communicate purpose when it has so many ways to be communicated via decisions, progress meetings, celebrating wins, navigating crises and so many other ways that purpose is referred to and communicated.

If you listen to leaders of purpose-led organisations, they will often tell stories or make comments that reflect their purpose. When they are interviewed in the media, or when they need to make a tough call, they will communicate a form of their purpose in the context of that situation. It might be different words, but it has the same meaning every time and can be done in many ways, at many levels at different times.

Here are some ways that purpose is communicated:

- Formal communication of the purpose.
- Welcome emails to new hires that inspire and affirm the purpose.
- Stories in hallways and meetings that explain it in action.
- Celebrations of when it is achieved.
- Referring to it in decisions, especially tough ones.
- Acknowledging behaviour that is consistent with purpose and using that as an opportunity to communicate and reinforce purpose.

The goal here is to continually communicate your purpose. You simply cannot communicate a purpose enough—especially if you are driven by it.

Step 3: Demonstrate

It is easy to demonstrate purpose when things are going well. But the most powerful and credible demonstration of purpose is the decisions and actions you take when things are challenging.

In 1982, Johnson & Johnson discovered bottles of Tylenol had been tampered with and laced with cyanide in a Chicago pharmacy. They took immediate and decisive action. Instead of trying to downplay the situation or prioritise profit, they prioritised customer safety. Despite significant cost, the company immediately recalled 31 million bottles of Tylenol nationally and rapidly developed an industry-leading triple tamper-evident seal. Johnson & Johnson stayed true to their purpose of caring for the health and well-being of their customers, which regained public trust and restored the brand's reputation.

Another example is when Starbucks faced a crisis in 2018 when two Black men were arrested at a Philadelphia store for not ordering anything while waiting for a friend. Starbucks could have downplayed the incident as isolated and unfortunate, following up with a standard public relations apology and left it at that.

Instead, Starbucks closed over 8,000 stores across the U.S. for a day to conduct racial bias training for all employees. The company met with the men involved and worked with civil rights leaders to improve their practices. By taking these actions, Starbucks demonstrated its commitment to civil rights, and to their purpose "To inspire and nurture the human spirit", even in the face of criticism.

I have a story of my own. Years ago, I took a senior sales leader role and after a few months, it was clear that salespeople needed support on a number of fronts. They were being held back by underperforming parts of the organisation, and their own peers, that they depended on to make sales. Simply pushing salespeople for better sales figures was not the answer. My purpose became clear: it was NOT to grow sales— my purpose was to grow salespeople. I did this by growing their skills, clearing red tape, boosting morale, teamwork and commitment with those they worked with. It worked as we grew sales quarter on quarter. However, my purpose was put to the test when one of my direct reports, a sales director, chose to bully rather than grow their salespeople to get results. As some of our best salespeople started jumping ship and HR complaints flooded in, the hard decision to dismiss the sales director became clear and easier when it was anchored to my purpose of growing (not bullying) salespeople.

All business decisions should be anchored to and relate back to purpose. They are made clearer by purpose. They are easier to justify and explain when made in reference to purpose, especially when they are difficult situations or decisions.

STAGE 3: MEASURE

As mentioned earlier, purpose is correlated with performance under certain conditions. A purpose that generates results must be clearly articulated, meaningful and integrated into your organisation's operation and culture.

To ensure your purpose is effective and getting results, the final stage in implementing purpose is to measure it across three key areas that are correlated with performance.

1. Integration

Do employees know the organisation's purpose?

Do employees believe that customers know the organisation's purpose?

2. Meaning

Are employees inspired to take action to achieve the purpose?

Do employees feel proud of the organisation's purpose?

3. Integration

Are decisions and behaviours consistent with purpose at all levels in the organisation? Is the meaning of your purpose continually referred to in internal and external communications, decisions and actions where it makes sense? Are people able to make decisions to enact and demonstrate the purpose? Are your people acknowledged for their achievement of purpose?

For purpose to be effective, you need to measure it

This model will help you determine how effective your purpose is. You can measure it yourself or use the 5 Factor Assessment developed for this book which integrates purpose with all of the 5 Factors. The goal is to find areas where your purpose is working, and where the gaps and opportunities are to leverage purpose for greater business performance.

The Bottom Line

Creating a world-class purpose statement for your organisation is essential in becoming unstuck and accelerating results.

Many of the world's well-known high-performing organisations have achieved exceptional results with their purpose.

Studies show that in many organisations, most employees are disconnected from the purpose of their work.

There are 3 steps to creating a purpose that works: articulating it, integrating it and measuring it.

Articulating a purpose involves making it personal (we need to care and be proud of it), making it commercially viable, and making it meaningful (time to get real, specific and actionable).

Integrating a purpose involves aligning strategy, decisions and actions with your purpose, then continually communicating and demonstrating your purpose in the real world.

Measuring your purpose ensures that people understand it and are proud of it, are empowered to achieve it and that decisions and actions are aligned with it.

Factor #3
Customer-Centricity

Every one of the world's high-performing organisations studied had a razor-sharp focus on customer-centricity. If there was one thing that helped them outperform their peers, it was customer-centricity.

Customer-centricity is a strategic and cultural orientation that places the customer at the centre of a company's decisions, operations, and ideas. It is more than good customer service. It is a fundamental shift in prioritising and aligning your organisation's strategy and operations around customer needs.

The goal of customer-centricity is to create customer value. Your organisation already creates customer value otherwise it would be out of business. However, many organisations have become stuck by competing organisational agendas, misalignment and differing focus across teams. Their focus on customer value has faded and so has their momentum and results.

History is filled with failed organisations and leaders who took their focus off customer value creation. They all fell behind, became irrelevant or were replaced because they couldn't generate results as well as they once did.

The key to unlocking results is to refocus on customer value. Prioritising customer-centricity will accelerate how your organisation operates, drives efficiencies and creates value both internally and externally. It will highlight unnecessary obstacles and conflicting goals that currently slow your organisation down.

As you will see in the upcoming chapters, the world's high-performing organisations don't give customer-centricity lip service, they set the standard for it. Customer-centricity is a major factor in their high-performance.

8

What is Your Customer Centricity Strategy?

Customers are the reason any organisation exists. It doesn't matter whether your organisation is a not-for-profit, a government agency or a corporation. If you remove the customer, your organisation has no reason to exist.

Customer-experience is a competitive differentiator. It is how disruptors disrupt. It is how organisations grow and how they shrink. Under-serve your customer and your organisation will underperform.

Customer-centric organisations perform better. The statistics are overwhelming. Customer-centric organisations are 60% more profitable. Their employees are 1.5 times more engaged. Their customers are loyal, being 5 times more likely to buy again, they will pay 17% more for products and are 4 times more likely to refer friends.

Their higher performance is logical. Costs come down due to fewer complaints and problems; customer acquisition efforts and costs are lower; operational efficiencies go up. Employees are more motivated by a customer-centric culture; they become more invested; willingly collaborate to solve problems and improve how they work.

Customer-centric organisations are also more innovative within their industries. Look at Apple, Tesla, Amazon, Lego and many of the other organisations studied. They are all leading their industries. It is no wonder that 81% of organisations view customer experience as a competitive differentiator.[8]

These are some of the key areas and considerations the world's high-performing organisations have:

1. Focus on Customer Needs and Expectations

Customer-centric companies prioritise understanding and meeting their customers' needs and expectations. They invest in learning about their customers' preferences, pain points and experiences, to offer products, services, and experiences that truly meet their needs.

2. Personalisation and Customisation

These businesses often use customer data to personalise interactions and tailor their offerings to individual customer preferences. This might include personalised marketing, customised products, or individualised customer support.

3. Feedback and Continuous Improvement

Customer-centric organisations actively seek and value customer feedback. They use this feedback to continuously improve their products, services, and overall customer experience.

4. Empathy and Understanding

Customer-centricity involves empathy for the customer, understanding their perspective, and effectively addressing their concerns, which results in trust, confidence and loyalty.

5. Employee Engagement and Training

In customer-centric organisations, all employees, not just those in customer-facing roles, are trained and motivated to consider customer needs in their work. This creates a company-wide culture that supports customer-centricity.

6. Long-term Relationships Over Short-term Gains

Customer-centric businesses focus on building long-term relationships with customers rather than prioritising short-term profits. To protect long-term profits, they will prioritise customer satisfaction and loyalty over a short-term cost.

7. Integrating Customer Centricity into Business Strategy

Customer-centricity is not a separate department or a role, it is woven into the entire business strategy. This means aligning product development, marketing, sales, delivery and customer service around the needs and experiences of the customer.

8. Responsive and Proactive Customer Service

Providing excellent customer service is a key component of customer centricity. This includes being responsive to customer enquiries and complaints as well as proactively addressing potential issues. High-performing organisations empower their people to make decisions that serve customers while protecting their interests.

9. Technology and Innovation

Many customer-centric organisations leverage technology to enhance the customer experience. This can include the use of CRM systems, data analytics, AI, automation and self-serve technologies that better serve customers. However, many organisations implement technology with the aim of saving time and money. This can frustrate customers if the customer experience was not designed into the technology to start with. High-performing organisations implement technology with the customer in mind and with the goal to benefit both the customer and the organisation.

10. Consistency Across Touchpoints

Consistency in customer experience across various touchpoints (in-store, online, customer service, etc.) is crucial in a customer-centric approach. This consistency helps in building a reliable and trustworthy brand image.

High-performing organisations aren't just talking about customer-centricity, they're leading the way with innovative strategies that are linked to ROI.

Here's a peek into how some of the world's high-performing organisations are redefining the game:

- Patagonia sends employees on "immersion trips" to use their products like their customers would so they can truly understand their needs.
- Ritz-Carlton empowers employees to intuitively anticipate and solve customer problems before they arise.
- Spotify music selections are based on individual listening habits. Netflix are using AI to curate content that shows an understanding of customer needs.
- Amazon have "working backwards" teams with members from different departments designing products and services based on customer needs, not internal constraints.
- Southwest Airlines employees participate in customer feedback sessions, then collaborate across departments, including flight attendants and mechanics, to decide how to improve customer service.
- Zappos' employees have the freedom to go above and beyond to delight customers.
- Southwest Airlines flight attendants are empowered to make decisions to delight customers, like giving impromptu upgrades.

- Whole Foods Market's store teams have autonomy to tailor offerings to local tastes and preferences, instead of a one-size-fits-all customer offering.

These are just a few examples, but they showcase how leading organisations are leveraging the customer-centricity factor. By obsessing over needs, personalising experiences, empowering employees and embracing feedback, they are reaping the rewards in all four metrics: financial growth and profitability, employee engagement, and customer satisfaction and loyalty, and leadership in their industry.

Considerations for a Customer-Centric Strategy

Business Strategy
Implementing customer-centricity requires changes in the way an organisation is run. If you don't have a customer-centricity business strategy, you are giving customer-centricity lip service.

Processes and systems
The use of systems and processes other than surveys is available to understand customer needs.

Collaboration
Cross-team collaboration is required to assess data on customer needs and real-time experiences—and to create an end-to-end customer experience that spans multiple departments.

Empowered employees
To deliver excellence in customer experience, employees need to be empowered. They need authority to make decisions that resolve or enhance customer experience. And they need training in the **business of empathy** discussed in Chapter 4.

Customer-centricity often requires a Customer Experience (CX) leader who spans multiple functions and has the backing of the CEO and executive team. The CEO will often set a shared customer experience goal at the executive team level, led by the CX leader.

The CX leader will then implement several objectives across functional units such as using omnichannel experience, proactive empathy, data collection and predictive analysis, planned employee empowerment, feedback mechanisms, AI-powered personalisation programs and employee immersion programs.

Accelerating cross-team collaboration to achieve rapid results on shared goals is covered in Chapter 20 – Creating a Collaborative Environment.

The Bottom Line

Organisations that are stuck have often lost their focus and priority on the customer.

Customer-centricity unlocks both financial and performance gains. It engages and aligns employees, leading to optimised resources, budgets and results.

Many organisations see customer-centricity as a key factor in their success. Their senior executives lead company-wide efforts to create customer experience.

Customer-centricity is increasingly important in today's competitive business environment, where customers have more choices and higher expectations.

Companies that successfully implement a customer-centric approach can differentiate themselves and build a loyal customer base.

The key to becoming customer-centric is to make fundamental cultural changes in what the organisation focusses on.

The remaining chapters in this section outline the fundamental shifts to harnessing the power of customer-centricity for results.

9
Work Backwards from the Customer

Having a focus on customer experience is how start-ups like Lyft, Uber and Airbnb became successful. It is how disruptors take market share from once dominant organisations. Their focus is on serving a customer need better than it is currently served or taking advantage of an industry where customers are underserved. Maintaining a strong customer focus, as Amazon does, is how organisations come to dominate.

Amazon creates their success by using a process they call "Working Backwards". The main idea is to start with the intended customer experience and work backward to design the product or service. It is a rigorous process that gets deep into the detail before a decision is made to bring it to reality.

Amazon product teams write the press release before designing and building the product. This challenges them to work backwards from the customer's experience, answering why it is different, better and will delight the customer. An example is the Kindle's press release on customer experience. It is often quoted as: "You can think of any book and be reading it in 60 seconds". This approach of imagining and writing the press release before designing the product creates customer experiences that are more profitable, more relevant and more efficient to produce.

When Jeff Bezos was Amazon's CEO he said, "If there's one reason we have done better than most of our peers in the Internet space over the last six years, it is because we have focused like a laser on customer experience, and that really does matter, I think, in any business."

The result: Amazon's Kindle and Prime customers shop more frequently and buy more expensive items on average[1]. Amazon's financial success is clearly linked to the customer experience created by their products and services.

This focus is not limited to high-tech or young organisations. The 95-year-old company Unilever is known for its priority on customer experience.

They actively use digital channels to interact directly with customers, responding to enquiries, feedback and product development requests. Their responsiveness and direct connection with their customers distinguish them from competitors who are less active and connected with customers. They invest heavily in R&D, developing product features from customer requests and quickly adapting product offerings to evolving trends. Organisations are never too large or too successful to move quickly in response to customer needs.

Apple has been surpassing all customer experience standards for decades. Their current NPS is the best in their industry—scoring 72 vs an industry average of 54.

Apple's process is worth replicating. Steve Jobs was obsessed with creating a great customer experience through great products. He believed that products, not profits, should be the motivation because it changed the way decisions were made, which people you hired and the eventual profits that followed. He eventually learned to balance profits and products—but he had them in the right order from the start. Great products create great profits. And in Apple's case those profits are large. The largest on the planet.

It is not a case of creating great products and hoping people buy them. Jobs explained that Apple didn't start with a particular technology or product and hope customers would buy it—instead Apple starts with the customer experience, then works backward to design the product, then the profit. It is the priority and sequence that Apple follows that makes such a huge difference.

Apple's sequence: 1. Customer Experience
2. Product
3. Profit

This is different from the traditional, numbers-based approach. Most organisations start by looking for pockets of unrealised revenue and then work out what to sell. This is the opposite of working backwards from the customer. It is working backwards from profit and putting the customer last.

A traditional sequence: 1. Profit
                         2. Product
                         3. Customer Experience

Capturing pockets of unrealised revenue is good business, but putting customer experience last is short-sighted. It is counter to innovation and sustained performance. It is an important distinction that makes a huge difference to how an organisation is run. History has shown us that many once successful organisations that eventually failed put profit first and customer experience last.

Outside-in vs Inside-out

When an organisation starts with customer experience, they take an outside-in approach. However, when an organisation starts with profit, KPIs or other performance numbers, they are taking an inside-out approach.

Organisations lose momentum when they become preoccupied with themselves and lose contact with changing customer needs and preferences. They also waste resources and time trying to satisfy their own chiefs rather than their customers. They eventually lose relevance, become stuck, bloated with unnecessary bureaucracy and, in some cases, begin a decline that ends in being taken over, sold or broken up.

The traditional sequence of Profit > Product > Customer leads to a failure to innovate. It blinds leadership to important strategic changes needed to survive, and instead leaves them riding old revenue streams for too long.

In the past this focus has left many companies like Kodak, Blockbuster, Borders Books, General Motors (although back now) and Nokia either out of money or irrelevant.

Even the mighty Microsoft started to lose relevance by taking an inside-out, numbers first approach. In the early 2000's, Microsoft missed many crucial tech trends, falling behind organisations like Apple and Google. Microsoft grew revenues by relying on and riding existing revenue streams of Windows and Office but failed to innovate in mobile, search and cloud, losing their leadership position and putting their future in question. When Satya Nadella took over in 2014, he revamped Microsoft with an outside-in approach, making it a major player and innovator once again.

Nokia was not so lucky.

The Story of Nokia - Losing Momentum & Relevance

Nokia was an organisation caught by a focus on profit numbers and a belief that their momentum and market position would last for years—but eventually (and unexpectedly) it slowed down and then stopped entirely. How they didn't see it coming was a mystery to me at the time.

When I was consulting to Nokia in the USA a few years before the iPhone was released, Nokia was the best-selling mobile phone brand in the world. They had the best-selling mobile phone of all time in 2003 (the Nokia 1100), but smartphones were coming. The BlackBerry had just been released. It was great at messages but poor at web browsing. Palm and Windows smartphones were confusing and clunky. Their tiny screens used an old (resistive) tech that often required a few presses to detect a finger and needed a stylus for some functions. And Nokia's phones were not very "smart" with limited apps and basic web access. Customers expected a more desktop-like experience on their mobile device. There was a HUGE opportunity waiting to be met.

I remember asking some of the North American Nokia executives what their vision of the smartphone market was. They said they were still working it out.

Then in 2007 Apple introduced the iPhone. It instantly exceeded customer expectations, leaving every other smartphone in the dust. Apple had started with the expected customer experience, then designed the product, and then worked out how to make a profit.

Despite Apple's success, they only had 5% market share while Nokia had 50%. Nokia had huge R&D resources and funding at their fingertips, but they apparently had the wrong approach. In 2009, Nokia released the N97 dubbed the "iPhone killer" but it was a failure because it didn't meet customer experience expectations. Its touchscreen was old tech compared to the iPhone and so were its apps. Nokia appeared to have started with profit and not with customer experience.

When the N97 failed, Anssi Vanjoki, Nokia Vice President of Markets revealed that Nokia's focus was on profits before customer experience when he said the N97 had absolutely met the company's goals for sales volume and revenue, but it was a "tremendous disappointment in terms of the experience quality for the consumers and something we did not anticipate".[24]

Over the next 5 years, Nokia's value decreased by 90% and was acquired by Microsoft in 2014—interestingly a deal made under Bulmer's leadership, which turned out to be a failure that cost Microsoft billions.

How the world's best mobile phone company lost everything is often discussed in business schools, but here is the bottom line: Nokia had huge resources but didn't use them wisely. Nokia could have gained a serious lead over competitors in the new smartphone category. Instead, they rode the old revenue streams of their existing and once successful mobile phones for too long. Then when the iPhone was released, Nokia appeared to use an inside-out approach—focusing on how many N97 phones the could ship quickly and how much money they could make. Nokia was focused on profits not customers. Their operating profit in 2003 was around $5 billion vs Apple's tiny operating profit in the tens of millions.

The tables turned because Apple focused on customers and profits in that order. Nokia, by their own admission, had it the other way around.

Studies [7] of Nokia's demise found that:

- Nokia front-line workers and middle managers were too scared to tell the truth about the limitations of their products and what they thought customers wanted. The Smartest Person in the Room Syndrome.
- Managers were driven by fear of missing quarterly targets. Micromanagement instead of Hands-on Leadership.
- Top managers bullied middle managers to be more ambitious to meet their goals. Middle managers then lied to top managers.
- Managers did not feel safe to challenge top managers nor were they empowered to act on what they thought was right.
- Top managers were not hands-on enough to understand their people, the technology and customer needs. This affected their ability to set direction and the right goals. Hands-off, data without detail, and numbers-focussed leadership.

In contrast, Apple employees who had developed the iPhone from their CEO down were known for being:

- Tech literate and attentive to the details required to innovate.
- Focussed 100% on the user experience before the technology.
- Hands-on in a way that united people to achieve the right goals.

- Their hands-on, customer-centric approach allowed them to leapfrog market leaders like Nokia and BlackBerry.

It appeared that Nokia's prior success made it hungry for more success and more money at all costs. Running with an inside-out approach, internal competition between divisions created an aggressive and unproductive environment that former employees have called a madhouse.

Nokia ultimately suffered from managers' need to protect their own jobs and meet KPIs rather than focus on customer needs and work backwards to profit. Their leaders were not customer-centric or hands-on and did not foster an environment where people were free to speak up or challenge ideas.

The Bottom Line

Customer-centricity is creating customer value by working from the outside in, starting with customer needs and working backwards to products and profits.

The world's high-performing organisations don't give customer-centricity lip service, they set the standard for it.

As Seth Godin once said, "Don't find customers for your products. Find products for your customers."

A focus on customer experience keeps your organisation connected to trends and customer preferences. It allows you to maximise returns while continuing to stay ahead.

Prioritising customer-centricity will accelerate how your organisation operates, highlighting unnecessary obstacles and conflicting goals that currently slow your organisation down.

Whether you are a not-for-profit, government agency or corporation, your customers are the reason your organisation exists.

Customer-centricity isn't a nice-to-have. It is essential for high performance and survival.

As customers, we all want a great experience. But are we giving our customers a great experience? If not, why not?

10
Encourage an Outside-in Focus

A root cause of becoming stuck is people being focussed on the wrong things. As seen in the previous chapter, the world's high-performing organisations achieve customer-centricity by encouraging an outside-in focus. However many organisations that have become stuck have an inside-out focus.

Awareness of why this happens is often enough to encourage a return to an outside-in focus.

When organisations are formed, they focus on understanding customer needs. They adapt quickly to produce products and services to meet those needs. This is an outside-in focus.

As organisations grow, their focus changes to creating stability and structure to scale and meet demand. Functional departments are given key performance indicators (KPIs) to measure their effectiveness. Managers then seek to optimise their department's performance. People inside the department begin to focus on achieving their KPIs and serving their manager and KPIs. This creates an inward and upward focus. People focus inward on their own success and upward to serve their manager or senior leadership. This can become a huge distraction and drain on productivity and results.

People who should be working together start working against each other to achieve their own goals. Everyone is focusing on their own needs without really focusing on what the customer needs. Time that could be spent serving the customer is wasted on ass-covering and infighting. This dynamic works against the organisation's overall goals.

When this happens, the organisation has lost its outside-in focus. It has become focused from the inside out. This leads to a disconnect with the customer and the essential purpose and identity of the organisation. Business can rely on existing momentum, but only until growth slows and the organisation begins to stagnate.

The Business Cycle of Stagnation to Decline

As business begins to stagnate, instead of focusing on creating customer value, managers become preoccupied with numbers. Over time they become disconnected from their customers, their products and eventually their operation. This leaves them without enough insight to lead with confidence. Products and services begin to date because old revenue streams are relied on for too long. As a result, customer experience drops, customers spend less and they look to competitors for better value and service.

The business shifts from stagnation to decline— management commences rounds of desperate downsizing where budgets and people are cut. Initiatives that defy common sense are attempted. The good people leave. Employees who were proud of the organisation's reputation become bored with the obsession on numbers above all else. Staff turnover, quiet quitting and minimum effort follow.

Organisations like this are frustrating to work for. They are frustrating to buy from and deal with. They have lost their focus on the big picture and the reason they existed in the first place. They open the door to innovative competitors who will happily take their customers, revenues and best talent.

Leadership can dramatically improve organisational performance by encouraging an outside-in focus. Much of this book is aimed at achieving this focus by defining a clear purpose, turning managers into leaders who are hands-on and support their people to serve their internal or external customers. Leaders must remove conflicting goals and unnecessary bureaucracy and controls so people can achieve better results, faster.

The Bottom Line

An outside-in focus is a return to the focus an organisation had when it started.

The Problem:
Many organisations, despite good intentions, shift their focus from customer needs to internal metrics and bureaucracy. This inward focus leads to decreased productivity, employee dissatisfaction, and ultimately, stagnation and decline.

The Root Cause:
The root cause is a loss of the "outside-in" perspective, where the organization prioritises its own internal processes and goals over the needs of its customers.

The Consequences:
A loss of customer focus leads to an eventual decline in productivity, customer satisfaction and results. This leads to desperate downsizing and cuts to budgets, resources and capability. This ultimately creates a toxic work environment with low morale, high turnover and lower output.

The Solution:
To reverse this trend, organisations must re-establish an "outside-in" focus. This involves empowering employees to prioritise customer needs, removing

bureaucratic obstacles, and fostering a culture of innovation and continuous improvement to achieve strategic goals.

The Role of Leadership:
Strong leadership is crucial in driving this cultural shift. Leaders must set a clear vision, inspire their teams, and create an environment where employees feel empowered to make decisions and take risks.

Encouraging an outside-in focus starts with defining who the customer is. There's an old saying that "If you're not serving the customer, your job is to be serving someone who is". Everyone in an organisation has a customer. This focus enables the world's high-performing organisations to achieve better results faster.

11

Idiot Machine!

The third cultural shift in becoming customer-centric is how you engage and empower people in your IT department. The increasing speed at which new technologies are developing makes empowering your IT department more important than ever.

Many IT projects fail to deliver on expectations. They also frustrate customers and businesses, running over budget and producing solutions that do not work as expected.

In the context of customer centricity, there is a simple mindset change required to fully leverage the benefits of new technology. This is especially important with the emergence of AI and other technologies that can potentially help or harm an organisation faster than before.

While I was living in the USA, I travelled to Paris to help General Motors with a high-level software rollout plan for Europe. Every morning, I was picked up from my hotel and driven to the office by Thomas, one of their finance executives.

Thomas had a direct style of communicating which was very French. I found it amusing and insightful because he called it how he saw it.

Each morning, like a scene from a comedy sketch, Thomas would stop next to the access terminal for the parking garage. He would roll his window down and give the machine a withering gaze, as if to say, "You again?" After a tap of his security card, the machine would emit a reassuring beep, only to leave the garage door unmoved.

Thomas would then slap his card on the machine's face like a glove slap, challenging it to a duel. Beep. Nothing. Beep. Zilch. Beep. Nada. It was like a musical instrument stuck on the same note. After another 3 or 4 faster and slightly harder taps, the access control terminal would decide to allow us entry, playing the same beep as before but opening the door this time.

"Idiot Machine!" Thomas would mutter in his French accent as he drove us into the garage.

This story isn't just an isolated incident – we are surrounded by idiot machines, seemingly designed and authorised by idiots.

In Australia and New Zealand, many airlines have reintroduced self-service kiosks at airports. They are new and improved! The idea is to improve customer experience by making it simpler, faster and less stressful than standing in line for an agent.

You know how it works. You simply take your bag to the machine, print and apply the luggage tag, and the machine scans and takes your bag. You're then free to go into the airport and relax.

For whatever reason, the last 3 times I have used the self-serve kiosks the idiot bag machine refused to take my bag. The last trip I was extra careful to put my bag and luggage tag perfectly in front of the scanner. Maybe this time? Nope. It just would not scan the tag. I was thinking I was the idiot. Maybe I had put the tag on wrong? Then an agent came over. She looked senior. After 3 long minutes of moving my bag to the left, to the right, turning it around and around, the idiot machine refused to scan my bag and take it.

I said to her, "These things don't work very well do they?".

"Tell me about it," she said. "I hear that hundreds of times every day".

She motioned toward the service desk, "Follow me, let's do this the old way" and took me to the counter, checking my bag in less than 30 seconds.

The self-service kiosks may work fine 90% of the time, but they do glitch. The point is that technology is only great if it works better than the thing it replaces. Not 90% as well or even 100%. It must work better. I have spent my career in technology and business and love new gadgets, but if they are hard to use or don't work, they won't get much use.

Forcing customers to use technology that frustrates them is bad for business. They can see that the organisation isn't 100% committed to their customer experience. They will tolerate the glitchy experience but will become indifferent to the brand or, worse, resent the brand. Is that really what any organisation wants? It is commercial suicide.

Why is it so hard?

The problem is NOT that we don't have the technology. I could build a better, more reliable luggage scanner in my garage with a 5-year-old PC, a $30 USB barcode scanner and some duct tape (and maybe a 14-year-old kid to develop the app).

Whether your airport experience is the same as mine or not, I am sure you have used badly designed technology—confusing parking meters; complicated websites; info buried deep inside company intranet pages; stupid self-service sites to log IT support requests; microwave ovens that won't start; and TV remotes with so many buttons you start smacking them on the arm of the sofa to get the sound to turn down. Next will be poorly implemented AI not working as expected.

The problem is not the technology—it's the people who develop the technology. They are not really focused on the customer experience. Not because they don't care and not because they are idiots. They are very smart people—specialists employed to make hardware and software work together. They are called IT And they are set up to fail.

Why IT Projects Still Fail

Most organisations plan and execute technology projects by tossing them over the fence to IT people. IT are rarely given a business strategy or much guidance on the end-user experience. They are treated separately from the business and tend to behave separately, controlling only what they can control with limited autonomy and authority.

This might have been okay when Information Technology (IT) did what its name implies—produced information like sales or debtor reports for businesspeople to manage their business. Today IT is not only transforming organisations; it is often the main point of contact for customers who interact with our technology.

Business can no longer view IT as separate.

Organisations need to combine IT specialists with businesspeople who understand the customer experience from start to finish, especially when they cross multiple departments and technologies.

Even with the use of Agile and experienced IT project managers, IT projects still fail. Over 51% of 400 US firms surveyed said they have seen no increase in performance or profitability from digital transformation efforts in the past 2 years.[2] Several other studies report similar numbers that fail to deliver on expectations.

Many tech projects are aimed at saving money when they could transform the way a business works but won't happen without collaboration and agreement with the people in the business to change the way they run their business. Instead, technology is overlaid onto a business that hasn't really changed. The result is a disappointingly long and expensive exercise and things that are largely the same as before.

The common reasons for technology projects failing are straightforward:

1. Lack of real empathy and focus on customer experience
2. Unclear accountability for outcomes of technology
3. Weak Collaboration
   a. Not involving all departments and functions in design and planning
   b. Not collaborating in person (causing delays and misunderstandings)
   c. Disjointed collaboration between business operations and IT
4. Lack of purpose and sponsorship from executives who are not hands-on enough to set shared goals for technology initiatives.

Layering new technology over disjointed or misunderstood processes without end-to-end ownership of the customer or user experience simply doesn't work.

In business more than ever, technology is viewed as a competitive advantage. This is incorrect. It is not the technology that is the competitive advantage; it is how you use it that is the competitive advantage.

Technology, like product design, should start with customer experience and work its way back to cost savings or revenue and profit growth.

The Bottom Line

The rapid pace of technological advancement offers a huge advantage to become unstuck and get results faster, yet many IT projects fail to meet expectations, frustrating customers and exceeding budgets.

Many examples highlight poorly designed technology, such as glitchy airport kiosks and frustrating user interfaces, demonstrating a lack of focus on the customer experience.

A common reason is that IT departments are often isolated from the business, leading to misaligned projects and a lack of understanding of customer needs.

Organisations often prioritise technology itself as a competitive advantage, rather than how it will be used to enhance customer experience and business outcomes.

The solution is a fundamental shift in mindset toward customer experience to leverage new technologies, particularly with the rise of AI, which can significantly impact an organisation.

The Role of Leadership:
Foster stronger collaboration between IT and all departments, ensuring shared ownership and

accountability. Strong executive sponsorship and active involvement in technology initiatives. Focus on desired business outcomes of technology projects as well as the human interaction and customer experience for increased productivity and satisfaction.

Factor #4 Fully Empowered People

E mpowering people does not come naturally to many organisations. As pressure on leaders to get results goes up, it is natural for them to implement controls to manage risk and drive results.

The problem is that this often disempowers people by putting obstacles in their way by removing authority and adding rules and tasks that slow people down. Any organisation can relate to this with the addition of industry regulations that disempower and slow them down.

Almost every organisation is calling for less red tape, obstacles and complexity. Private sector organisations are urging governments to reduce complexity to streamline processes for applications, approvals and services. Governments are urging private sector organisations to innovate, improve employee productivity, streamline internal processes and improve customer experience to drive economic growth. Empowering people is the key to uncovering and removing unnecessary obstacles and complexity.

It is the fastest way to speed up outcomes and growth.

The operating models of the world's high-performing organisations are fast and frictionless. They empower teams with clear expectations, trust, autonomy and accountability. They manage performance and value agility. They constantly remove obstacles and seek simplicity.

Fully empowering your people is a decision to set clear direction, provide full support and then trust them to do their part while holding them accountable if they don't.

12

Nobody Wants to Suck

Many leaders I have coached tell me they are frustrated because they don't understand why people are not performing. When I outline the 4 reasons that people don't perform at their best, it all becomes clear. Before we get to those 4 reasons, let's dispel a popular myth about human behaviour.

We often make the mistake of thinking people are happy to be mediocre. When we are frustrated in the traffic by that useless driver in front of us, or the customer service person who doesn't seem to care, we tend to think it's them and not their situation.

In psychology, this is called attribution error. It means that we assume other people's performance is due to them personally, rather than their external circumstances. However, when we are not performing we are more likely to attribute it to our external circumstances. For example, when we are that driver who is holding everyone up, we can see that the cause is our circumstances not us! The GPS isn't working, and we are lost in a strange city.

As a leader, assuming people are happy being mediocre is not only an incorrect assumption, it is a limiting one. Think about it. Nobody ever wakes up in the morning, looks in the bathroom mirror and says, "I really want to suck today!"

But what about the quiet quitters, the slackers or the people who have no idea they are underperforming? That's where the 4 Reasons people don't perform are important.

The 4 reasons people don't perform at work are:

1. They don't know *what* is expected of them.
2. They don't know *how* to do what is expected.
3. They don't have the *tools* or *freedom* to do it.
4. They don't have the *desire* or *ability*.

The first three reasons above the line are the leader's responsibility. The fourth reason is the employee's responsibility. Let's apply these from a leader's perspective.

1. Telling people exactly what is expected of them.
Everyone has a different definition of success. What one person considers mediocre might be a significant achievement for another. For this reason, leaders need to clearly articulate what success looks like. This needs to happen for everyone, from the executive team all the way down to front-line employees.

Some leaders resist this idea because they don't like to micromanage. This is not micromanaging. This is setting clear expectations. It is like showing people the goalposts in football. If they don't know where the goalposts are, how can you expect them to score goals? Micromanaging is different—it is anxious managers trying to control every step people take toward achieving the goal.

It is also important to explain why. The concept of "why" popularised by Simon Sinek has always been the difference between people doing a job because they have to and doing a job because they want to.

Make no mistake, the importance of clearly articulating exactly "what" is expected cannot be understated. It creates individual responsibility and shows people the level of performance you expect.

2. Making sure people know how to do what is expected.

Leaders play a significant role in employee training and development. Technology, business and customer expectations are changing quickly. Ensuring people have the latest knowledge is essential to performance. It is also essential people know who to go to and how to get things done inside their organisation.

It is amazing how many leaders tell me that people should know how to do their job. In complex organisations it can be hard to know where to go and who to ask to get help or to get things done.

The best organisations I have ever worked for or consulted to place importance on training, coaching and mentoring. They make sure their people are well supported internally and that their knowledge of their job is industry-leading.

Many organisations like Apple ensure that their managers know the jobs their people are doing at least three levels below them. While this may not always be possible in some organisations, it is important for leaders to also hold some expertise and knowledge in the key aspects of the roles people below them are performing. That way they can provide training, mentoring and coaching.

3. Giving people the tools and freedom to do what is expected.

To achieve exceptional performance, it's critical for organisations to provide employees with the best tools to do their work. These are not just fit-for-purpose tools but tools that inspire and motivate people to do great work.

I once saw a salesperson from a large organisation using a laptop that was so old the battery had swollen and was making the back of the laptop bulge. The salesperson looked defeated, explaining that his employer refused to provide a new one. He said the battery only lasted 30 minutes. He was embarrassed to take it to clients and was afraid it might catch fire. This is a true and current story. How motivated do you think that salesperson was? It is short-sighted to save $1000 on a salesperson's laptop when that salesperson generates $2.5m in sales. I found out that the salesperson was one of about 50 people who had old, broken IT equipment.

Freedom is as important as tools in supporting an employee's performance. Freedom comes in two parts: removing obstacles preventing an employee from getting their work done and giving them freedom in how they do the work.

Giving employees freedom requires good leadership on the first two items above—being clear on what is expected and ensuring they know how to do it. Training on company values, ethics, policies and conduct, and how to do these things is essential.

It then gives employees the freedom to try new ideas or ways of achieving their goals. It allows them to make more decisions and be accountable for the outcome. Think of the opposite—removing freedom of choice, providing unfit tools and leaving obstacles in their way while expecting top performance is crazy!

Leaders, like great sports coaches, play an essential role in removing obstacles that prevent their people performing at their best. In business it is the act of prioritising the identification and removal of unnecessary obstacles and processes.

4. They don't have the desire or ability to do what is expected.

Once people know exactly what is expected, how to do it, and have the tools and freedom, the responsibility is then on them to perform. If people don't want to do what is expected and only want to do the minimum, they may have become quiet quitters or people who are in the wrong job. The short answer is that they need to go. This is a case of performance management which is made easier by good leadership in the first three reasons of why people don't perform.

If people are working hard but just don't have the ability to do what is expected, they need to move into a role that suits them. Once they are aware of how their performance does not match what is expected, they will sometimes choose to move. If not, the leader and organisation can help them find a role either internally or externally.

When leaders are skilled in these four things, they can benefit from what I call the Upside-Down Organisation, which I detail in Chapter 15.

The Bottom Line

Underperformance contributes strongly to organisations becoming stuck.

Leaders have a role to play in their people's performance.

3 of the 4 reasons for underperformance are within a leader's control.

Nobody wants to be mediocre. Even if they are.

People can't succeed if they don't know what is expected of them.

People can't succeed if they don't have the tools, freedom or training to do their job.

How are you setting expectations and supporting the performance of your people?

13

Trust Creates Performance

A lack of trust is the #1 reason organisations slow down and become stuck. It affects how people lead, how people follow and how people work together.

It doesn't matter how good your strategy is. It doesn't matter how good your people, or your products are. A lack of trust inside your organisation slows everything down.

Low trust means more rules, more layers of approvals, more time and more costs to get things done. The result: lower performance and lower results. Low trust makes people wary of sharing ideas and taking risks; they don't work together as freely or as efficiently. When trust is low, everything is slow.

If trust is present, it magnifies speed and results. It lowers costs, effort and time, and it motivates people to perform at their best. People like being trusted and they like being able to trust others.

Think about your relationships with key customers or partners in business. When there is a large deal on the table, if your customer trusts you the business happens quickly. If they don't trust you, the process is slow and more complex. You have to jump through hoops, prove yourself and earn trust before they will do business with you.

As a CEO or senior executive, the inference is clear — trust gets better results, faster. But how do you extend trust safely to safeguard results?

The good news is that trust can be restored and extended safely, and results will follow. It is one of the easiest things to fix that will move an organisation forward.

Here are three common areas of low trust inside organisations and how to restore it.

Low Trust Area #1 - Management not trusting people

When managers don't trust their people, it results in more rules and approvals that slow down everyone. Decisions become centralised higher up the hierarchy. Executives with low trust often hoard decision-making power. This disengages people, kills their enthusiasm and stifles innovation and excellence.

For example: a salesperson makes an error on a customer sales quotation. It costs the company the profit on the sale. This rarely happens as most salespeople are experienced in checking their quotes.

The head of sales responds by putting a new process in place. All salespeople must get their quotes approved by their sales manager. And if a quote is over a certain amount, it must also be approved by the sales director. You have seen what happens next.

The sales manager and sales director are flooded with quotes requiring their approval. They become a bottleneck for getting quotes out to customers who will buy from a competitor who is faster at getting them a quote. The managers are overwhelmed and spend less hands-on time supporting their team to perform at their best. They fall behind and out of touch with industry and product changes.

If they hire a sales administrator to help, costs go up. If customers receive competitor sales quotes first, revenue declines as sales are lost.

In this example, a lack of trust causes the organisation to slow itself down. It has also lowered what it expects of people. The expectation of performance has now dropped to the lowest level of performance—people who make mistakes on sales quotations.

The top-performing salespeople become frustrated because they are treated like the learners or lower-performing salespeople who make mistakes.

It is reasonable to expect salespeople to produce accurate quotes. The bar needs to be raised not lowered.

Don't lower your expectations to the lowest level of performance in a team. Set the bar at the level of performance you expect. Then train, support or relocate underperformers.

Restoring management trust in people

Five simple steps can restore trust while managing risk to speed up performance.

1. Set the bar.

Reassess what you expect of people. Check that you have not lowered expectations to the lowest level. What is reasonable to expect of people in terms of behaviour and performance? Next, tell people what is expected and what is NOT acceptable. Explain the consequences of not meeting expectations. The bar is set.

2. Match authority and responsibility with expertise.

Give authority and responsibility to the people with the expertise in a particular outcome. They are best placed to make decisions, manage risk and be held accountable. Holding decision-making power from these people just creates a bottleneck that causes people to get stuck

3. Trust people to do their part.

Let people know you are trusting them to do a task properly, and that they will be held accountable for their work. Remove controls and let them do the task. Do random checks to confirm things are being done and risk is managed.

4. Manage mistakes or poor performance when they happen.

Don't lose trust and don't blame. If it is not a dismissible offence, create a learning opportunity. Restate what is expected. Coach, train and provide tools. In most cases, performance will increase. People will respect and appreciate you.

5. Don't tolerate repeated mistakes and poor performance.

If mistakes, bad conduct or poor performance continue a second time, give people a warning. If they repeat the same thing a third time, consider removing them from the role. Don't reduce expectations, remove authority or add controls as this will hinder other people in similar roles.

Low Trust Area #2 People not trusting management

If people think they will be judged for an idea, a mistake or a failure, they won't trust management. They will not take a risk and make suggestions or try things to get great results. When things go wrong, people will keep things secret to avoid seeming like they failed.

Restoring people's trust in management

Make it clear that it is okay to make a mistake if you tried your best. Make it clear the focus is on learning not blaming. Make it clear that failing once is okay if people were trying their best. It is an opportunity to learn and improve. Failing twice at the same thing means more care is needed. Failing three times means their fit for the role or task may need review. This makes it clear people are accountable and supported to learn and succeed.

Some failures require immediate dismissal. Most have room for learning.

Low Trust Area #3 Teams not trusting each other

Lack of trust in a team or between departments will harm collaboration. Conflicting goals often cause conflicting intentions. This will result in people not trusting each other. The last thing you want as a leader is one team resisting another. It's like having the handbrake on in a car—the accelerator pedal is trying to move the car forward, and the brake is holding the car back.

Restoring teams' trust in each other

This is made much easier if conflicting goals between teams become shared goals. When teams have shared goals the focus is on improving achievement of the goal. The next cultural shift is to remove blame if one team lets another down. The culture to build trust between teams is to focus on finding solutions not finding blame. This gives people confidence to look for ways to improve their own work. We want people to admit problems or mistakes and not be punished for a one-off thing that we can learn from and improve. Improvement, not blame—is the name of the game.

The Bottom Line

Trust is a competitive advantage in an organisation. Those that have it work better together. They go the extra mile, try new ideas and take calculated risks. They don't get stuck!

With trust, there are less hoops to jump through. The advantage is speed, efficiency and lower costs—and people who are motivated to achieve their best.

High trust organisations are high-performing organisations. Many studies confirm this. Compared with low-trust companies, people at high-trust companies report: 74% less stress, 106% more energy at work, 50% higher productivity, 13% fewer sick days, 76% more engagement, 29% more satisfaction with their lives and 40% less burnout.[4]

Expect high performance and trust people to deliver it. When people fail to deliver, use it as an opportunity to learn and improve.

Don't stop trusting people. Remove people who have proven that you can't trust them.

14

Overcontrol Reduces Performance

Many organisations have implemented a centralised organisational structure. This is perfect for optimising shared functions, like IT and finance, but when decisions are centralised and taken away from business units it can have significant consequences on speed and results.

Centralised decision-making grew in popularity in the mid-2000s. It removed decision rights from managers and workers and gave a single leader, usually the CEO or senior executives, the power to make most decisions. On the surface, this idea seemed like a sensible control to manage risk and contain costs across large organisations and geographies. However, the trend to centralise decision-making often coincided with changes in the way senior executives were measured and paid.

For many leaders, centralised decision-making is the norm, but for others it becomes more than that. A recent study found that "power-hungry" leaders intentionally hoard decision-making rights for personal gain and largely "nefarious" reasons.[12]

Centralised decision-making in these cases was being exploited and has been found to have significant consequences for organisations.

Leaders that hoard decision-making rights end up disenfranchising and disempowering middle managers and workers. This impacts an organisation's efficiency, speed and results. For example, customer-facing people (think call-centres) without the basic authority to fix customer issues only manage to frustrate customers and turn them away. But worse, there is one other consequence the study found—Power-hungry leaders who retain many decision-making rights will go as far as to sacrifice the success of their organisation to ensure their own success and control.

It is probably only the minority of senior executives that go that far, but the point is that centralised decision-making has largely run its course—it is the old normal. It is linked with slower performance and contributes significantly to organisations becoming stuck. In many cases it negatively impacts the organisation's results and wastes senior executive energy and time.

The new normal is to devolve decision-making as far down the organisation as possible. It makes sense to allow those who are directly responsible, best positioned and qualified to make a decision – then to hold them fully accountable.

Most CEOs don't need to make decisions about more than a few key things that they own, such as strategy, culture, acquisitions, major capital investments and structures. They might get involved in or give an opinion on other decisions, but they don't have to make them, nor should they. If CEOs, COOs or the executive team are making too many decisions or are hoarding decision rights from people better placed to make the decisions, it is highly likely the organisation is moving slower, getting poorer results and suffering other negative consequences.

Devolved decision-making is central to the leadership style used by hands-on leaders to fully empower their teams in many of the world's high-performing organisations. The skill in leveraging this is to implement it effectively and safely with a structured methodology.

How-to Devolve Decision-Making to Empower Your People

How you devolve decision-making rights will vary from organisation to organisation. What will be common is the need to do it. Unless an organisation is in crisis, devolving decision-making and control is an excellent strategy for growth and faster results.

The starting point is to assess your organisation for opportunities to push decision-making as far down into the organisation as possible. To understand this assessment, you may want to engage a coach or consultant or use the 5 Factor Assessment Tool.

I have done this as a leader and as a consultant for many organisations. The first step is to decide who should be making the decision—this is the person who is directly accountable for the outcome – and then determine who else needs to be consulted and who needs to be advised about it. Doing this will reduce the number of meetings and people required to sign off. It will even increase the approval level of people lower down in the organisation when they are accountable for decisions.

When more than one person needs to be involved in the decision, it still comes back to who is finally accountable for it. Everyone else is and should be welcome to provide input and debate the best outcome. We covered creating an environment that encourages people to share ideas, debate them and allow the best ideas win in the chapter "The Smartest Person in The Room". The idea is that an executive may not be the person making the decision, but they and others can debate the best solution in a safe environment.

If a tiebreaker is required, the person who is accountable for the outcome will make the final decision—even if there is disagreement. This may not be the most senior person in some cases.

As an executive, I have held true to this many times. I disagreed with people below me on the approach they wanted to take but allowed them to make the decision because they were accountable for the outcome, and I gave them my full support. My role was to get out of the way and avoid being a bottleneck.

In a large organisation this is not a simple task to assess and change, but the benefits outweigh the costs of overcontrol and unnecessarily centralised decision-making.

The benefits of allowing the right people to make decisions are:

- People take more ownership of the outcomes
- Efficiency, speed and output will increase
- Customer experience and loyalty improves
- Leaders get more time for higher-value tasks

15
The Upside-Down Organisation

I want to share a personal story of how I create high-performing teams. I have done this for many years in different organisations. Early in my career, I realised that organisational hierarchy was important for reporting and accountability but not for empowering people to perform at their best. Empowerment needed an upside-down organisation.

This is the story of the upside-down organisation.

While working at SAP, I was asked to build a regional consulting practice in a newly opened satellite office. It had been isolated from headquarters and was growing slower than other regions.

When I arrived, there were a handful of consultants and a sales team. The consultants were frustrated by the conflicting demands on them. The local sales team were using them to provide free consulting to win sales, but the head of consulting needed them on paid customer projects implementing SAP software.

At the time, customer projects were run by the 'Big Four' consulting firms, with our SAP consultants assisting. The Big Four had hired a lot of consultants but many were fresh out of training. Our role was to ensure customer success by answering any questions about our software, advising and quality checking progress on projects to ensure customer success.

There was only one problem. My new team struggled to find their place on customer projects. The Big Four didn't want to give up consulting revenue so my team could provide advice. And customers didn't understand why they needed my team when they were paying a consulting firm to run their project.

This situation was frustrating and confusing my SAP consulting team. It became clear they were floundering. There were 4 things they needed:

1. A clear purpose
2. An identity inside and outside our organisation
3. Clear goals and guidelines
4. Control over their work
5. The support to clear the way for them

This is when I came up with the idea of the upside-down organisation!

The Upside-Down Organisation

I called a meeting with the new team to discuss all of this. I decided to start with clarifying the team's purpose. I drew this picture on a paper flip chart.

```
                    ┌─────────────┐
                    │     ME      │
                    └──────┬──────┘
          ┌────────────────┼────────────────┐
┌─────────┴────────┐ ┌─────┴──────────┐ ┌───┴────────────┐
│   Financials     │ │ Materials Mgt  │ │  HR/Payroll    │
│   Consulting     │ │  Consulting    │ │  Consulting    │
└──────────────────┘ └────────────────┘ └────────────────┘
```

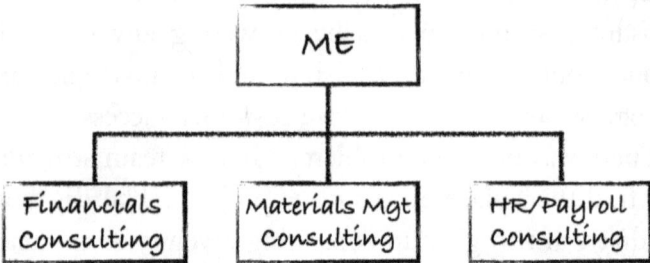

The basic org chart represented the 3 consulting practices in my team.

Next, I asked if anyone had noticed what was missing from most org charts?

I added customers to the org chart and held it up.

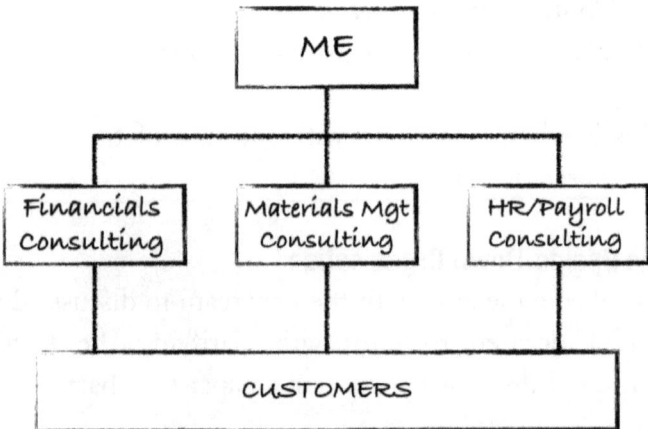

```
                    ┌─────────────┐
                    │     ME      │
                    └──────┬──────┘
          ┌────────────────┼────────────────┐
┌─────────┴────────┐ ┌─────┴──────────┐ ┌───┴────────────┐
│   Financials     │ │ Materials Mgt  │ │  HR/Payroll    │
│   Consulting     │ │  Consulting    │ │  Consulting    │
└─────────┬────────┘ └─────┬──────────┘ └───┬────────────┘
          └────────────────┼────────────────┘
        ┌──────────────────┴───────────────────┐
        │              CUSTOMERS                 │
        └───────────────────────────────────────┘
```

Then as a team we clarified our purpose, identity, goals, guidelines, control and support.

Purpose

I explained that their customers were their people. They needed to make sure they were successful. In that moment the team's purpose fell into place. Their purpose was to serve their customers (not me, not the sales team and not senior management).

Identity

While the Big Four consulting firms were implementing our software for customers, we (the vendor) were responsible for it working. Our role was to be the experts in our software, to ensure customer projects were successful. This meant supporting the Big Four when they got stuck and doing quality assurance checks on their work for our customers.

When my team heard this, there were nods and smiles all round. They now had a purpose and an identity.

Goals & Guidelines

I then explained that we had 4 goals: revenue targets to keep us profitable; customer satisfaction with our products and services; to be the best in the industry; and to have fun.

Once they heard these goals, they asked questions about how other regions were operating. I gave them clear guidelines on legal, financial and consulting processes for working with customers. Then we

discussed values and agreed conduct. There were 3
guidelines:

1. We would have each other's backs while on
   customer worksites. If we needed to debate with
   each other that would be done in private.
2. Any decision they made must benefit both the
   customer and our company.
3. We would always be proud of any action we took if
   our family or peers read about it in the newspaper.

With these goals and guidelines in place I gave them
creative control.

Control & Support

Each member of my team was a subject matter expert.
They had experience in their customer's roles, so they
were in a good position to advise them. They were now
becoming software specialists in those roles – finance
and accounting, logistics and HR. They had goals and
guidelines; now they needed freedom and control to
decide how they did their work. And they needed the
support to clear the way so they could get it done.

Turning the Organisation Upside-Down

I ended our meeting by turning the piece of paper
upside down.

I smiled and said, "This is how we are going to work
from now on".

```
┌─────────────────────────────────────────┐
│              CUSTOMERS                    │
└─────────────────────────────────────────┘
     │                │                │
┌──────────┐   ┌──────────┐   ┌──────────┐
│  HR/Payroll │ │ Materials Mgt│ │ Financials │
│ Consulting │  │ Consulting  │ │ Consulting │
└──────────┘   └──────────┘   └──────────┘
                    │
              ┌──────────┐
              │    ME    │
              └──────────┘
```

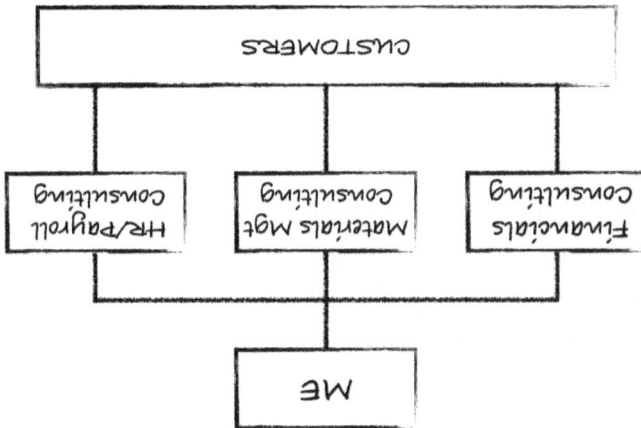

Then I explained, "Your job is to work for our customers and my job is to support you".

I said that I would remove obstacles getting in their way. I would also provide the tools and training so they could be the best in the industry. We discussed how we would make decisions. It came down to who was responsible. If you were responsible, it was your decision. Being responsible meant that if it went bad your job, not someone else's, was on the line. The buck would stop with you. However, if it meant they would lose their job and their immediate manager would also lose theirs, it wasn't their decision—it was their manager's decision.

This didn't frighten the team, it encouraged everyone to come up with great ideas and try them out. Mistakes were treated as opportunities to learn (not to be punished) with a guideline that the same mistake should not be repeated.

In the weeks following, I bounced the idea off my boss and his boss the CEO. They both liked it and pledged their support.

Record-setting success

Our original three goals were to: grow our revenue and profit; delight our customers and; be the best while having fun doing it. We smashed all three metrics: profitability, customer satisfaction and employee satisfaction.

We ranked as the highest performing region in the country—and in the top 10 out of 100's worldwide. We did it year after year, adjusting as we went.

The Bottom Line

The upside-down organisation is a vertical alignment from the top down. It is a leadership shift from controller to coach. It required hands-on leadership at every level. It stops teams, departments and organisations from getting stuck.

A leader's role in the upside-down organisation is to:

1. Re-enforce their team's purpose: To serve their customers
2. Define team identity: What they own, control, excel at and are proud of
3. Agree team goals, guidelines, conduct and values that are real
4. Provide tools, training, feedback and support
5. Remove obstacles and get out of the team's way

16
You're No Fun

Something has gone missing in many workplaces. It's a sense of enjoyment and fun at work. Maybe it's due to post-pandemic fatigue, maybe it is growing workloads, too many tasks and meetings and not enough time, maybe it's outdated leadership. Maybe it's all of that, but in the process, we lost something and we need to get it back.

We need to recapture that sense of enjoyment and fun for ourselves and our people. There are always parts of work that are not fun, but that doesn't mean we can't make time and space for fun.

Having fun at work is counterintuitive to some leaders. It appears like slacking or goofing off. Hands-on leadership gives people clear goals and purpose. These leaders manage people who underperform and support them to perform at their best. Part of that is creating an environment where both top performance and enjoyment are encouraged.

Now, I could justify this with research and statistics but that's not as much fun as a personal story.

One of my early mentors was the late Ken Katzenberger, the head of consulting at SAP Australia. Ken knew how to make work fun and enjoyable while getting great results. And he had a big influence on my leadership approach and success.

Ken was sent to Australia by the CEO of SAP America to reorganise the fast-growing consulting services business. He had strategies to scale the team, grow revenues and profit, and lift customer satisfaction —but his first play was to build morale, pride, teamwork, and a sense of fun and enjoyment.

One of the things I always remember about Ken was that he was fun yet professional. He knew exactly what to do, had a ton of fun doing it, and still managed to remain professional, ethical and collaborative. His mantra was, "Hey guys, we take our jobs seriously, but we don't take ourselves too seriously".

He was always quick with a joke or a witty remark that made you feel good while keeping you focused on the goal. He encouraged us to look out for each other, to take time to share experiences in the hallways and kitchen, and to take pride in a job well done. Most consulting businesses would frown on this because they are focused on one thing: trying to maximise billable hours with customers rather than chit-chatting in the hallways wasting valuable time.

Ken knew that fostering a sense of fun and comradery was a performance booster—it gave us energy, confidence and enthusiasm. Our meetings were often about telling stories before reviewing numbers. We celebrated successes and discussed mistakes. Rather than punish mistakes, Ken reframed them in a positive and sometimes humorous way in front of the group. Call it learning through laughter or error correction with a smile; Ken used fun to enhance performance. He set group standards in a way that everyone felt motivated, not chastised.

Our performance spoke for itself. We were an innovative group who were one of the most profitable in the 100-plus countries SAP operated in.

We enjoyed finding ways to do things better, lifting profits and customer satisfaction on our projects, sharing new knowledge and having fun along the way. It was energising and fun most days, and on tough days we had each other and a laugh or two.

Ken was a maestro who combined pride and fun in the pursuit of excellence. He also made sure he developed a group of future leaders to take over when he went back to the US. Luckily for me I was one of them. His approach of making space for fun while taking pride in your performance left an indelible mark on me that produced great results in the teams I led and the leaders I have coached.

Stories aside, there are many statistics and studies showing the value of fun and enjoyment in the workplace. It is measurable and so is its impact.

In any organisation, if you measure employee engagement along with enjoyment you will see a correlation. Low scores in one will be matched with low scores in the other. Add innovation, creativity and discretionary effort (more than required) and you will also see scores that match engagement and enjoyment.

When enjoyment is replaced with anxiety, discontent and overwhelm, how easy is it for you to think creatively or positively? And how motivated are you to put in extra effort, beyond what it takes to get a pass mark, when you feel like that?

The Bottom Line

If we're asking people to perform their best at work, to go the extra mile, why would we offer them anything less than an enjoyable time doing it?

In the same way we maintain physical equipment, we need to maintain people. Fun and enjoyment are essential maintenance for people's sustained performance.

How could you make space and time for fun at work?

20 minutes of fun can significantly improve an afternoon's work results and stop people from getting stuck.

How could you create a culture that takes work seriously but doesn't mean taking yourself too seriously? One that encourages performance and enjoyment.

17

Remove Unnecessary Obstacles

Jeff Bezos CEO of Amazon often said: "Anytime you make something simpler and lower friction, you get more of it".

If you want your people to do more, make what they do simpler. Remove unnecessary friction and complexity. The place to start is removing unnecessary obstacles.

Large organisations commonly experience unnecessary internal obstacles. Many of them fly under the CEO's radar or have become 'business as usual' so that no one questions the obstacles.

This is an enormous and almost instant opportunity for organisations to become unstuck! Organisations can instantly save time, money and lost talent by removing unnecessary obstacles.

The most common unnecessary obstacles are:

- Redundant processes, causing duplication and complexity
- Approvals and signoffs, causing bottlenecks and lack of accountability
- Broken handoffs between departments, causing rework and error
- Poor communication, wasting people's time in emails and meetings.

As organisations grow, they need structured processes to streamline work, manage risk and comply with laws and regulations. The problem is when processes start to become unnecessary obstacles. There are three causes of rules and processes becoming obstacles to performance.

Cause #1: Managing Risk vs Over-Controlling

Risk needs to be managed, but overcontrolling for risk and failing to manage underperformance is where things start to go wrong. When an employee does the wrong thing, a manager has a choice: manage the individual's performance or introduce more rules (such as approvals or extra levels of signoffs) that restrict everyone.

In most cases the solution to managing an employee who has done the wrong thing to set or reset clear guidelines, trust them to do their job BUT to performance manage them when they don't. However, many organisations simply add more rules that slow everyone down (and frustrate the good employees who are trying to get results faster). It lowers people's spirits and demotivates them over time.

It is the same frustration a CEO or senior executive feels when regulators introduce a new external rule because another organisation did the wrong thing. Regulators are killing organisations and their ability to get ahead, yet organisations do the same to their people by adding rules internally just because there was one bad egg who did the wrong thing or made a mistake. This is making organisations get stuck!

Solution #1: Assess risk, then trust and manage people

Decision-making authority can be devolved as low as possible when the risk is matched with the appropriate owner. The owner of a decision must have the required experience, be fully accountable for the outcome, and be properly trained and motivated to make the right decision.

Here's an example of devolving decisions as low as possible in a large organisation. Salespeople report to sales managers who report to sales directors who report to the sales VP. Who should decide which salesperson is hired under a sales manager?

It is not uncommon to see a sales VP incorrectly enforce their decision on the sales manager because all sales roll up to the VP's target achievement. But this is putting the decision too high and disempowers the sales manager. The VP should have input, and so should the director but the manager a) has the required experience, b) is accountable for the salesperson's performance and c) is properly motivated to make the right decision. While the sales VP may be responsible for all sales, the risk of one salesperson not working out is smaller to the sales VP but it could be huge for the sales manager. Also, the sales VP may not have the local knowledge of the sales manager's customers and needs.

A much simpler example is travel requests. I have seen managing directors retain approval for ALL travel requests in a 2,000-person division. That is not only a huge drain on their time, but it also creates a decision bottleneck and demotivates managers and directors.

The key here is **letting go** of control, **trusting** people while **managing** performance.

A great number of operational decisions should be devolved to give lower-level employees the authority and accountability for decisions they are best equipped to make. Executives free up their time to focus on decisions that span functions, strategy, culture and major financial and legal moves. Many decisions do not require multiple steps or approvals and can be monitored or audited.

There are other frameworks such as RASCI (Responsible, Accountable, Supportive, Consulted, and Informed) that help define who and how many people are involved in decisions.

During COVID-19 many organisations made good decisions and produced desired outcomes in days instead of months. This is possible if there is a focus on shared goals, trust and commitment.

Cause #2: Accepting the Status Quo

Many organisations are restricted by ghosts of the past. Obsolete steps and rules that were put in place may no longer necessary. These often cause unnecessary work that can be quickly eliminated on closer inspection of the work people are required to perform to get a task done. The problem is that most people have given up complaining that a rule or process is a waste of time.

In most organisations if you ask anyone, "Why do we do it this way?" they will say, "That's how we do it" or "It has always been that way", or "We just have to do it because they're the rules." When this happens an organisation is most likely stuck. They are not improving or refining how efficiently they work. This gives senior leaders little room but to use blunt instruments like budget cuts and layoffs to achieve time and cost efficiencies. In many cases this may weaken an organisation's ability to execute to achieve results faster.

Solution #2: Challenge the status quo to justify itself

Early in my career I spent years helping organisations simplify business processes to take advantage of automation software. Software like this is often built to contain the best-practice processes, but 90% of the time the organisation I was helping had a different, more complicated process. This revealed the number of obsolete, redundant and broken processes. Many of them even defied logic and common sense.

The way to reveal obsolete, redundant and broken processes is to simply allow people to question why a process is done.

An example is Elon Musk's email to Tesla employees encouraging them to identify and voice stupid rules: "If following a 'company rule' is obviously ridiculous in a particular situation, such that it would make for a great Dilbert cartoon, then the rule should change…please send a note."

To achieve this, here is a simple "process" to assess the validity of processes:

1. People need to feel comfortable challenging a process. Good ideas can come from anywhere. Invite people to speak up.
2. Every part of a process needs a logical, quantifiable reason for existing.
3. If that reason is:
    a. Unknown; there is an immediate opportunity to remove it.
    b. Can be achieved a better way, that avenue should be pursued.
    c. To control or avoid mistakes, that should also be questioned. Is control worse for performance than managing infrequent mistakes?
4. If a process is broken, the breakpoint should be identified and repaired by someone who is responsible for repairing it end-to-end.

5. If a process is obsolete, it should be immediately removed.

Cause #3: Poor communication

When departments don't communicate, they operate their own processes in silos. This can cause broken processes and hand-off errors between departments. People dealing with angry customers often have to chase other departments and do unnecessary extra work because of poor communication.

Long emails are often unnecessary obstacles.

It is common for people to write an email rather than call someone. They will write long emails that cost the reader time to read and understand when a short email, phone call or conversation would have worked faster. Often people will copy other people on emails that don't need to read them, further wasting their time sifting through a long list of unnecessary emails.

Unnecessary meetings create obstacles.

They are often scheduled because of poor communication. Like email, too many people are included and the agenda is often unclear and long-winded. No one likes to sit in a meeting listening to irrelevant information or decisions they cannot add value to. Fewer meetings would be called if people had more decision-making authority.

Managers often waste multiple people's time.

I used to go to a meeting with my peers to give a 10-minute update to my manager. Then I would sit there for another 50 minutes listening to the other 5 people give updates that were completely irrelevant to me. The manager spent an hour that was relevant to them but wasted 6 people's time for the 50 minutes they had to listen to their peers. It would have been better to do the meetings 1-on-1 only asking people to spend 10 minutes with the manager. Instead of 7 person-hours being wasted, it could have been 1 hour for the manager plus 1 hour for the 6 people combined. That's 2 total person hours of 7. That's a 70% reduction in wasted time in one weekly meeting. Imagine how much work you could get done spending 70% less time in meetings.

Solution #3 Insist on shorter, clearer, relevant communication

In the spirit of brevity, read the causes above and remove those behaviours. After that, help your people improve their communication or work with a coach or consultant to help you improve communication.

The Bottom Line

Most leaders are not fully aware of the extent of unnecessary obstacles holding their people back. Leaders can and should seek to remove obstacles.

Many rules and processes are ghosts of the past. They are redundant controls and rules that can be removed to speed up results but have been accepted as "the way we do things around here".

Allowing people to question and improve how they do things is a huge shift in fully empowering people. It is based on a belief that given a chance people will change and improve how they work.

As discussed in the previous chapters, people want to succeed, they want clear guidelines and goals, but they also want support to achieve them. We need to trust people to do their jobs, but when they don't, we need to coach them or move them on, not add more obstacles and rules.

Communication is a huge timewaster and creator of unnecessary obstacles. Emails and meetings often create an unnecessary drag on time and performance.

The Role of Leadership: Getting started on this is simple. Ask people where the obstacles are. What is slowing them down and making them stuck. Visit the operation and get hands-on. Where there is empathy there are fewer obstacles. If you can see and understand them, you will quickly remove them.

For more complex processes, you need a way of assessing risk end-to-end, assigning owners and ranking changes by lowest effort and highest return. We discuss this in the last section of this book in Putting it all into action.

Factor #5
Cross-Team Collaboration

Collaboration is essential to executing an organisation's operating model—that is, how an organisation creates value for its internal and external customers, leading to increased speed, performance and results.

But not all collaboration is good collaboration. Some collaboration is bad. It wastes people's time, lowers performance and distracts people from the most important priorities. People can attend too many meetings, send too many emails and share too much information without questioning why or what the overarching priorities are. Attempting to collaborate without clear or agreed direction is bad collaboration.

Good collaboration is organised. It has an agreed set of priorities that everyone is aligned with. People will collaborate best when it directly moves the needle on agreed priorities. And when they are empowered and accountable to do their parts. Good collaboration is working together to achieve results that could not be achieved by working alone.

The difference is astounding. The time and money saved, combined with the increased performance, is worth the effort to improve cross-team collaboration.

Fortunately, this is easier to do than most people (and management consultants) think! But a different approach is needed.

In this factor we look at the common obstacles to collaboration that exist in many organisations. We take a new approach, based on the practices shared by the world's high-performing organisations. I have used these myself as an executive in a leadership role, and as a business coach when helping organisations improve collaboration for greater performance and results.

Creating highly collaborative teams is 100% within the control of leadership.

18
Herding Cats

"It's like herding cats!" is a frustration I hear when I am coaching leaders who struggle to get their teams working together.

It's true, cats are notoriously difficult to herd. They are not herd creatures who operate in groups and social structures. They are solitary, territorial and don't rely on each other for survival. They don't follow a leader and are driven solely by their own desires.

Humans are unique. We are both individual and herd creatures. We form social structures like families and work teams to facilitate cooperation. Human survival has historically depended on cooperation. Early humans hunted, gathered and protected each other in groups. These days we want to belong to a group we believe in and identify with. We still rely on cooperation with others to achieve and survive. **But here's the catch: we are also individuals with goals, desires and ambitions.**

In the right environment, humans are a collaboration superpower. We have explored outer space, created medicine, technology and engineering feats that have advanced our species massively. Organisations should be the perfect environment for collaboration. They have hierarchy, social connections and are organised around specific goals that result in success and survival. **But here's another catch: when our goals conflict with other people's, collaboration gives way to conflict.**

In organisations this is the definition of silos. We see misaligned goals and conflicting priorities between teams, often with unclear roles and responsibilities to each other. Silos are barriers between people who should be working together but are working against each other for survival—and the achievement of their own goals.

Silos create an unnecessary drag on performance. And it's worse than most of us realise. Studies show that leaders at the top of organisations are less aware of, and underestimate, the lack of collaboration and its drag on their organisation. When we measure how an organisation is collaborating, leaders are surprised at the unnecessary barriers and conflict that are slowing performance.

There are a few common reasons that teams don't collaborate.

- Even though different teams and departments depend on each other, it is not clear how they should work together
- They don't have agreed roles and responsibilities to each other

- Over time, teams have received individual goals and incentives that conflict with those of other teams
- With no cross-team coordination, people will focus on achieving their own goals before others' or the organisation's overall goals.

Efforts to increase collaboration often fail because the environment people work in does not support collaboration. There is an intention to foster collaboration, but the environment motivates people NOT to collaborate—teams are often rewarded for their individual, isolated success, which in some cases comes at the expense of organisational success.

How do we create an environment that supports collaboration?

It turns out we solved this over 100 years ago. We did it with project management. The most collaborative environment I have ever seen is a project environment.

Project management creates an environment where diverse teams have worked together to achieve the most amazing feats in human history. It is how NASA coordinated complex and diverse teams to put a man on the moon. It is how SpaceX transformed the aerospace industry; how Disney was created; how Apple put themselves five years ahead of competitors with the original iPhone; and it is how many of the world's high-performing organisations are reinventing and creating value faster than anyone else.

What is a project environment?

A project environment is a group of people from different teams working on a shared goal with a fixed timeline. Everyone's success is based on the same metric: successful project completion. A project is a shared goal.

Each team has objectives and tasks that roll up to achieve the project goal. For example, the goal of the original iPhone project was to create the first smartphone with a finger gesture touchscreen that was a fully functional phone, internet device and music player. That meant different objectives under that goal for each team. The hardware team needed to create the touchscreen. The software team created the apps to allow you to drive the screen with your fingers. And each team was responsible to another team. The hardware team depended on the software team to make the touchscreen work.

Projects are managed with weekly progress meetings to solve problems and track progress. The environment is highly collaborative because there is clarity around the goal, the timeline, the roles and responsibilities and the objectives and tasks required to achieve the project goal.

Collaboration is essential both for projects and for today's complex, fast-moving organisations.

A project environment depends on 5 elements to create collaboration:

- Collaborative Leadership Across teams
- A Shared Goal with a Fixed Timeframe
- Clear Roles & Responsibilities Between Teams
- Shared Metrics and Incentives Across Teams
- Regular Cross-Team Progress Meetings

How is this different from how we operate today?

Most organisations operate in process environments not project environments. Process environments are repeatable, stable, business as usual (BAU) tasks with people doing their job in their department.

Unlike a project environment, teams in a process environment focus only on their function and part of a process. When their part is done, they have achieved success regardless of the outcome at the end of the process—which is often the achievement of an overall strategic goal.

For example, a strategic BAU goal of ABC Toilet Paper Corp is to increase repeat business on their Supersoft Toilet Paper product. The goal is given to the marketing department. If the marketing department increases repeat business that quarter, they have done their job? Yes. But is the strategic goal achieved? Maybe not.

What if, the same month, the delivery team were asked to reduce shipping costs? They begin using a slower but cheaper delivery service. The extra sales generated by the marketing team overload the new delivery service causing delays to customer orders. Customers become disappointed (especially since this is Toilet Paper) and start buying from a competitor who delivers on time. As a result, repeat business declines.

The strategic goal (of increasing repeat business) has failed. Yet each team in the short-term has been successful. Marketing initially increased orders. Delivery reduced costs. But after a few months repeat business declined.

It's a simple example, but you get the picture: There was no collaboration between the departments on a shared goal. It is an example of siloed goal setting that creates misalignment and an environment that prevents collaboration.

The alignment created by a project environment solves problems like this. It also drives better end-to-end outcomes faster. It can save time and increase organisational effectiveness exponentially.

Project and process environments can coexist. Organisations do not need to drastically change their structures to do both. Strategic goals can be fed into project environments along-side business as usual processes and tasks. It does not require radical changes that you are not ready for such as organisation-wide use of project methodologies like Agile. All that is required is the use of a project management approach.

The world's high-performing organisations run the entire year this way—their goals are carefully selected, aligned across departments and run to a timeline within that year in a collaborative (project) environment. The same environment can be created in any organisation.

Project environments are exciting. There is a strong sense of team spirit, engagement and dedication. People work harder for the huge degree of satisfaction gained when milestones are achieved and projects reach a successful completion.

At the rate of change today, strategic goals need tight coordination, alignment and a sense of urgency that comes naturally from teams collaborating in a project environment.

The key is creating a collaborative environment that works for your organisation using features of a project environment.

The Bottom Line

Herding cats is difficult. Herding humans to work together is much easier. It is a key leadership skill made easier with a project environment. You'll find it used by the best project managers, CEOs, founders and leaders of disparate teams.

The Role of Leadership:

1. Commit to creating a collaborative environment
2. Start by measuring the current level of collaboration in your organisation
3. Then use a project management approach
   a. Create shared goals and timelines across departments and leaders
   b. Ensure that all teams agree clear roles and responsibilities to each other
   c. Incentivise everyone (appropriate to their role) on the same goals
   d. Run regular cross-team progress meetings—starting with the exec team

If you look closely at many of the world's high-performing organisations, you will find a project environment supporting and driving their strategic goals.

19
Avoiding Common Challenges

Many organisations attempt to create collaboration but are surprised when their efforts don't produce the results they expected. Before attempting to create a collaborative environment, it is important to avoid the common challenges that sabotage collaboration.

In my experience working with, consulting to, and studying organisations in different countries and cultures, there are four common challenges that hinder collaboration: People are unintentionally motivated NOT to collaborate; people don't know how or who to collaborate with; culture and communication are siloed; and Leadership is not clear on collaboration.

CHALLENGE #1:
People are unintentionally motivated NOT to collaborate.

There are a number of actions that unintentionally motivate people not to collaborate.

Siloed KPIs and incentives.

When KPIs and incentives are set separately at individual and department levels, it creates a very narrow focus. People become so fixated on hitting their own targets that they stop working together, cut corners and even harm other departments' results. It shows up as people not responding to requests from other departments or being slow to reply; not sharing information that others need; doing only their part; handovers between departments not being done or are done poorly; and a general reluctance to help people in other teams and departments.

A few years ago the US Navy identified that if called upon, they did not have enough jets ready to engage and win a potential fight. The numbers were at 40-50% and needed to be at 80% readiness. This meant a massive increase in performance was required and many thought it was not possible without more resources and money. But they did not have that luxury —they needed to reduce budgets every year going forward.

The only option was to identify obstacles and find new approaches. One of the major obstacles was the engineering department fighting for resources with the supply department, each focused on achieving their own metrics. When they removed the conflicting metrics (and applied the other approaches covered here in Factor #5 which are common to other high-performing organisations) they not only achieved their target, they exceeded it and then sustained it.

Cross-functional outcomes without a single point of ownership.

Accountability is essential to objectives and outcomes that span functional units. When these kinds of outcomes are owned by committees or multiple managers they often fail.

Trying to optimise one department in isolation.

Attempts at optimising one functional unit often come at the expense of overall organisational efficiency if done in isolation without any cross-team collaborative goals and management.

One of my clients was trying to reduce costs across the board while driving new sales. The sales team's goal was to generate new sales. The partnerships team's goal was to create partnerships that lead to new sales. The partnership team sponsored research in universities. In return the university would treat my client as a preferred supplier. When this was originally created, it was a great collaboration between the partnerships team and sales team to grow sales (not to mention a great external collaboration with the university). A problem arose when the CEO asked the partnership team in isolation to reduce costs. The CEO gave the VP of partnerships a KPI and bonus on reducing costs. The VP of partnerships had his team run the numbers and found that the university had not spent much with them so far that year. Without hesitation the partnership team visited the university and cancelled the partnership, explaining it was not financially viable.

Earlier that day, the university had placed an order for $2.1 million with the sales team and had committed to an additional $3 million order next month. The combined sales of $5.1 million far exceeded the cost of the partnership at $180 thousand. The orders were not yet closed in the sales forecast system, and the partnerships team did not consult with the sales team. They had just raced ahead to achieve their singular KPI and bonus.

Regardless, a lack of collaboration between the sales and partnership teams had put both sales orders in jeopardy. The company saved $180 thousand and almost lost $5.1 million in new orders. Luckily the sales team reversed the decision, but it doesn't always work out that way, and often decisions like this go unnoticed until it is too late.

It is common for siloed target-setting to undermine collaboration and have serious consequences on the larger business goals and results. Functional units that work independently without a shared understanding of their contribution to the core business goals often negatively impact the organisation's performance.

Competition for resources.

When different teams are competing for resources, such as budget or headcount collaboration will stop. People will compete rather than help others. Without some sort of relief for giving budget or resources to another team, people will compete aggressively to survive. This kind of competition is destructive to an organisation and is the opposite of collaboration.

I have seen so many situations where resources could be shared and relief on budget or KPI's given to one team so another team can succeed for the greater good.

For example: An aircraft grounded for days, costing over $700,000 in lost flights to save the engineering manager's P&L a $250 hotel bill to send an engineer to that city to fix the plane. If the engineering manager could cross-charge the $250 hotel bill to the ticket sales department, the company would have saved $700,000 in lost sales.

CHALLENGE #2:
People don't know why, how or who to collaborate with

Low awareness of other teams' expertise, needs and dependencies.
Many people do not understand the dependencies between their department and another. Every team in an organisation has at least one other team who depend on them. One team's output is another team's input.

There's an old saying that "If you're not serving the customer, your job is to be serving someone who is". A team without a customer is a silo. A team's identity and expertise are worth nothing if they don't serve an internal or external customer.

Unnecessary rivalry.
An old leadership trend was to encourage competition between people in an organisation and to reward

individual success. The belief was that the best people would rise to the top and the low performers could be removed. This had the unintended consequence of breeding a culture of unnecessary rivalry between people and departments.

It is common to hear things like "Those idiots in legal" or "Those jerks in sales". This is the LAST THING you want to hear as an executive leader because many strategic initiatives require collaboration across multiple functions to be successful.

An example is IT support. Many organisations give IT a KPI on how many support tickets they close. The problem is that this metric motivates IT to close tickets, not solve problems.

One of my clients had this problem—A salesperson raised an IT support ticket because their laptop display port was broken and explained they had an important sales presentation to make the next week. The IT person said there was no budget for a new laptop or a repair and closed the ticket. The salesperson raised another support ticket, this time calling the IT person to complain "I really need this resolved! This sales deal is worth over a million dollars to our company." The IT person hung up on them and closed the ticket. The salesperson had to cancel the customer sales presentation at the last minute. This is a true story that caused the loss of a sale worth more than the cost of a laptop, in fact it was worth more than an entire fleet of laptops.

The IT department were clearly working to meet their own KPIs rather than serving their (internal) customer and giving priority to the organisation's shared goal. The organisation had a strategic goal of getting a new product into the market to increase market share and revenues. Sales were pursuing the strategic goal, but IT were prioritising closing support tickets and reducing their department's expenses. This is a classic and true example of an organisation that still had pockets of inside-out focus.

This happens more than many executives realise. And yet they have the power to create a culture of collaboration with relative ease.

People can't find the right people, information, process or IT systems.

In large organisations it is common for people not to know where to get help. It is a huge drain on collaboration because people either can't connect or waste their own and other people's time trying to find out how to.

Too much generic collaboration distracts from targeted collaboration.

A common challenge organisations face is too many meetings and too many emails. People are drained and time-poor. On closer inspection (and if they are honest), many of the meetings that people attend don't have clear objectives and outcomes. Many of my executive coaching clients who are time poor have found that the objectives of regular meetings had been lost over time. The same was true of emails and being simply copied for information.

The idea of collaborating for the sake of collaborating is overwhelming people and lowering performance. This type of generic collaboration can be significantly reduced and replaced by a project, goal-based collaborative environment.

CHALLENGE #3:
Culture and communication are siloed

People not willing or able to ask others for help.
People are often willing to help but there is a culture of doing it yourself. This shows up as people not reaching out to other teams or departments for help. They don't collaborate because the culture is not to ask people in other departments for help. Conversely, people don't feel they have to help people in other teams.

One organisation I was brought in to create greater engagement and performance suffered from this.

There were hundreds of people in different teams with different roles and knowledge. Together there wasn't a problem they couldn't solve. The challenge was that they never asked the other teams for help, despite all being under enormous pressure to perform. After watching this for a while, I got them all together and gave them a pep talk. Essentially, I said, "You all have a lot of pressure on you to perform. From today onwards, none of you are in this alone. No one will sit alone at their desk sweating over how they will succeed or fail. There is an enormous depth of knowledge here across your teams. Starting today, it is okay to ask others in other teams for help or to bounce a problem around.

The solution is out there. You can ask anyone on any level. You can ask your boss, your colleagues, and even me. You are no longer alone. And remember, this goes both ways: you ask for help and you give help when asked. Let's meet again in a month to review."

There was a sigh of relief. People came and thanked me. They trusted that we would support and encourage this. And it worked. People worked together rather than on their own with problems they couldn't solve.

No cross-team progress meetings.

There are so many meetings in organisations, but most are not the kind that are conducted in a project environment. Project meetings track progress (against shared goals), address problems and come up with solutions. They don't bore people with information overload or irrelevant content. People don't turn up to the meetings wondering why they are there or what the meeting is about. They are highly focused, collaborative meetings of people committed to the same goals, timelines and outcomes.

People don't feel safe to collaborate.

Trust is a big obstacle to collaboration. Leaders need to trust people to do what is expected of them. When people don't feel trusted, they stop taking small risks like sharing ideas, trying new things or sticking their neck out in meetings with opinions and solutions. Collaboration requires open communication.

People need "psychological safety" to trust that they can identify problems, ask for change and challenge others in the spirit of getting the best idea or result. Peers need to trust each other to collaborate effectively. Creating psychological safety is easier when people are not divided by conflicting incentives and goals.

Hands-on leaders make it safe for people within and across teams to collaborate. They create a culture of working together to solve problems rather than assigning blame.

CHALLENGE #4:
Leadership is not clear on collaboration

Functional units and departments are not united by a shared goal from the top of the organisation.

In most organisations, strategic goals are broken down into individual department goals. This often causes a narrow focus that can create silos. One of the key challenges to collaboration within most organisations is people focused on their own goals, not working together on a shared goal. Siloed goals create siloed behaviour.

Collaboration starts at the top of an organisation; without it an organisation will never work well together. If there is one challenge to avoid before attempting to increase collaboration, it is to remove internal competition. Some organisations still encourage teams to compete against each other and not work together. This type of culture is outdated in today's complex and fast-moving business environment. The Hunger Games was a fictional dystopian teenage story. Competition within an organisation is often a waste of time, energy and resources. It is NOT how the world's high-performing organisations manage to generate top performance. They collaborate at the very top of the organisation and ensure that it continues all the way down to the front line.

Leading people to collaborate around shared strategic goals starts at the very top. The CEO is the team captain setting the strategy, priority and focus on shared goals. The exec team must be clear about and committed to collaboration; specifically, how their teams will collaborate to achieve the organisation's strategy. Leaders must demonstrate communication, behaviour and management of people that is consistent with collaboration.

In organisations with poor collaboration, members of the executive team run off with their own ideas and initiatives. They don't work in a simple project environment where the goal is shared and the objectives and tasks are divided up and managed as a group. When this happens, leadership is not clear on collaboration.

Some leaders need to learn to collaborate.

Another reason that leadership can be unclear on collaboration is simply that they don't know how to collaborate. Some individuals never learned how to collaborate. They reached senior roles by being competitive, or they were never required in their role to be collaborative in the first place. When senior leaders are not collaborative, there is a real problem that needs to be addressed. The losers are the CEO (and the Board), their customers and employees who, for the most part, want to collaborate.

This is more common than people think. Functional or department leaders often tell their CEO what they want to hear, then prioritise their own team's success at the expense of doing what's right to achieve the organisation's overall goals.

It is essential to get the right people on the executive team. Leaders who will unite around the shared strategy and set of goals; who will ensure their teams at every level are willing to work together on the goals set at the top.

Apple, Facebook, Google, Amazon, Tesla and others are publicly well-known for moving people out of roles when they prioritise self-interest over shared goals. These and many of the world's high-performing organisations depend heavily on collaboration across diverse and complex business units for their continued success.

There is no mechanism for feedback on hidden and unnecessary obstacles to collaboration.

A common mistake is executives thinking that everyone is working together or that their lieutenants are sorting it out. They stay at arm's length, unaware of obstacles to collaboration. Many organisations are not collaborating as well as they could or would like to. One reason is the hidden obstacles to collaboration (like those discussed above) and the other is people not having the confidence or ability to raise awareness of hidden obstacles.

Many employees believe that senior executives are not interested and expect them to "just make it work". In truth, senior executives want to know what is lowering productivity and impacting the achievement of strategic goals.

There is no measurement of collaboration.

The final reason that leadership is not clear on collaboration is that they don't have any data on it. Most organisations do not measure the effectiveness of their collaboration.

Fortunately, leaders can measure how well their organisation is collaborating, where the obstacles are and the opportunities to increase collaboration and performance. This can be done with generic 360 feedback surveys, or with the 5 Factor Assessment developed for this book which provides a collaboration score along with detailed scores on each area of collaboration.

The Bottom Line

When organisations do not collaborate within and across teams, they are stuck!

Attempts to foster collaboration often fail because of four common challenges that sabotage collaboration.

1. People are unintentionally motivated NOT to collaborate. Identify conflicting goals and penalties for collaborating. Align individual goals to the organisation's core goals.
2. People don't know how or who to collaborate with. Remind people who their customer is (e.g. legal supporting sales) and define expectations. Combine with shared goals.
3. Culture and communication are siloed. Create a cultural expectation and make it safe for people to ask for and give help. Combine with cross-functional team meetings on shared goals.
4. Leadership is not clear on collaboration. Collaboration starts at the top. Remove competition between leaders. Make all leaders accountable for organisational-level goals. The CEO is the Team Captain of collaboration.

Collaboration can and should be measured to identify obstacles and opportunities using your own assessment tool or the one developed for this book.

20
Creating a Collaborative Environment

The objective of creating a collaborative environment is not to collaborate more, it is to get better results, faster. Identifying the results you need will determine where you need to collaborate.

However, collaboration can get complicated, expensive and long-winded by taking on too much, adding too much and analysing every department and every process in the organisation. I am passionate about keeping things simple and easy to action, so the approach outlined here is much simpler. Sure, it will require effort but this approach is different. Instead of adding goals, processes and rules to drive performance, this approach subtracts goals, processes and rules to allow focus, performance and results to happen.

With a mindset of subtraction, alignment and focus, the organisation can become self-correcting as collaboration spreads. Is this a risky or disruptive change? No.

Creating a collaborative environment doesn't mean changing your organisation's structure. Organisations with functional teams like IT, Finance, HR, Legal, R&D, Product, Sales, Service, Delivery, Marketing Logistics and Engineering can create a collaborative environment using their current business model and structure.

However, creating a collaborative environment does require a project management approach. One that unites people around a shared goal, objectives and timeline. This is a proven approach to any undertaking where cross-team collaboration is required.

Rest assured that it does NOT mean implementing complicated project methodologies like Agile, Kanban, Lean or others if your organisation is not ready for them. Simple is good.

Let's get started. And let's keep it simple.

THE COLLABORATION FRAMEWORK

The following 5-step framework for creating a collaborative environment can be adapted to your own organisation and industry.

STEP 1: CREATE A UNIFYING GOAL

A unifying goal will unite everyone around a compelling and worthwhile achievement. People want to work for organisations that run this way. It attracts top talent and a high degree of engagement and effort.

The world's high-performing organisations run this way. The fast-paced tech firms like Facebook, Google, Amazon, Apple and Microsoft who constantly develop new products and innovations are well-known for creating collaboration with goals that everyone gets behind. Other high-performing organisations in diverse industries like Southwest Airlines, Netflix, Unilever and Best Buy have also achieved high degrees of collaboration around a unifying goal.

This type of goal is more descriptive than a vision statement and more compelling than an objective. It gives objectives context, meaning and purpose.

Let's use Qantas, Australia's national airline, as an example:

Qantas' vision is:
"To be a great airline that champions the Spirit of Australia."

Two of Qantas' business objectives are:
1. To overhaul the app to give customers more control over bookings, baggage tracking etc., and 2. To significantly expand the range of redemption options for frequent flyers.

Qantas's vision and objectives are good, but there is no link between the vision and objectives. The objectives sit on their own and don't really inspire people to work together to achieve them.

The objective to overhaul the app is likely seen as an IT job and not a priority for other departments.

However, there are multiple departments that could (and should) contribute to making the app amazing for customers. But what reason do they have? That's where the unifying goal comes in.

A **Unifying Goal** bridges the vision and objectives. It gives meaning to objectives and brings urgency and excitement to the vision. It is the reason and the worthwhile bigger picture that inspires people to work together and to do their best work.

Finding your Unifying Goal

The place to find your unifying goal is to start with an *important situation* your organisation faces.

Continuing with the Qantas Airlines example, following COVID-19, Qantas was accused of putting profits ahead of customers. Under the previous leadership, customers complained that they were sold tickets on flights that Qantas had already decided to cancel. There were many other complaints made by customers that Qantas has since taken seriously. Given this history, an example of an *important situation* for Qantas is damaged customer trust and loyalty.

Given Qantas's *important situation*, their unifying goal could be something like this:

> *Our #1 goal is to restore our customers' trust in us. We will make it easier and fairer for our customers to interact with our people and our systems to book flights, use points, check-in, fly with confidence and*

be treated with genuine care and the respect they deserve in the Spirit of Australia that defines our airline and our country.

This unifying goal connects the vision ("To be a great airline that champions the Spirit of Australia") and the objectives ("Overhauling the customer app...etc") by providing meaning and purpose that people want to be a part of and work hard to achieve.

Additional objectives could be developed that would engage and unite employees, such as: "We will empower employees to take initiative with customers, and to work together to keep our promise to our customers."

The **objectives** that come under a unifying goal are the actionable components to achieve the unifying goal. They are qualitative not quantitative outcomes that are worthwhile achievements such as, "overhaul the Qantas app", "significantly expand the range of redemption options for frequent flyers", "Create a top 10 list of discretionary customer decisions for flight attendants and ground staff", such as free upgrades for customers who are having a poor experience.

The **results and metrics** are then defined under the objectives. For the Qantas app, the metrics might be the number of new features, or exact metrics around how much faster or how many fewer keystrokes are needed to book a flight or to use points.

The Unifying Goal, Objectives, Results and Metrics fit together like this:

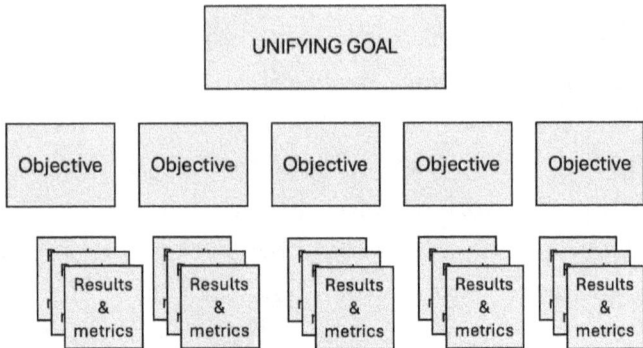

Examples of Unifying Goals in history

There is a degree of finesse required to create a unifying goal that will inspire people and achieve exceptional results. It takes an understanding of the most *important situation*, a keen insight into the people who you are asking to take on the goal, and a careful balance that creates value and meaning for the organisation and all its stakeholders.

When President John F. Kennedy (JFK) made his pitch to Congress to support the space program (and subsequent moon landing), he started with the most *important situation*. He explained that the Soviets had a lead on space exploration and the impact that could have on the freedom and confidence of Americans.

Next, he articulated a unifying goal, but he didn't simply say:

Our goal is to build a rocket that can go to the moon.

That statement would not have inspired a nation. It was but one objective in the bigger picture. His unifying goal was a far more worthwhile achievement. It was one level above the objective of building rockets.

This is how he worded his unifying goal:

> *I believe that this nation should commit itself to achieving the goal, before this decade is out, of landing a man on the moon and returning him safely to the earth.*

He outlined high-level objectives next, "We propose to accelerate the development of the appropriate lunar space craft... alternate liquid and solid fuel boosters, much larger than any now being developed...new engine development...(and) satellites for world-wide communication." And many other objectives like computer systems, space suits and other tech that didn't exist at that time.

He underlined the need for collaboration saying, "This decision demands a major national commitment of scientific and technical manpower, materiel and facilities, and the possibility of their diversion from other important activities where they are already thinly spread. It means a degree of dedication, organization and discipline which have not always characterized our research and development efforts. It means we cannot afford undue work stoppages, inflated costs of material or talent, wasteful interagency rivalries, or a high turnover of key personnel".

 This was a call to collaborate on a massive scale. And it worked. The moon landing and program remain one of the greatest achievements in human history by many teams of people working together.

  What about corporate example of a unifying goal? Maybe something a bit more down to earth?

 There are many examples of unifying goals that turbocharged cross-team collaboration to achieve exceptional corporate results. Disney's entire world of experience and content, Tesla's early lead in electric vehicles, Amazon's dominance of online retail, Apple's invention of the first fully functional touchscreen smartphone. They all had unifying goals.

 Everyone knows Apple, so let's look closer into their unifying goal when they invented the iPhone. It may have been the world's first smartphone with multi-gesture touchscreen and internet capability, but Apple's goal wasn't to develop a touchscreen smartphone for the internet. Their goal was, as they said at the time, "To reinvent the phone" which is exactly what they did —they reinvented the phone, as we knew it. To achieve this goal, it took hundreds of people in many teams. They not only achieved the goal, but they did it faster than anyone else, and they delivered it on time for the public release date. That is the power of a unifying goal that inspires people to collaborate and achieve exceptional results.

Beware of Goals that Backfire

Years ago, after merging with McDonnell Douglas, Boeing introduced an initiative called "ShareValue". They wanted everybody working together to increase the stock price. Technical teams, pilots, maintenance teams, everyone. Rick Ludtke, a Boeing employee at the time, said that even in technical meetings everything revolved around stock prices.[16]

Boeing's ShareValue was NOT a unifying goal for a couple of reasons. The first is that share value is not why people chose to work for, partner with and buy from Boeing. ShareValue is not what Boeing does for a living. Making it a unifying goal compromised the organisation's ability to create value that led to profits. One of the things this goal compromised was Safety. Aircraft failure can destroy a brand like Boeing, yet Boeing engineers and employees like Ludtke have gone on record saying relentless cost-cutting to increase share value sacrificed safety at Boeing.[17]

People want to work at an organisation like Boeing because they want to make advancements in aerospace technology that they can be proud of. A unifying goal that puts profit ahead of purpose isn't something hundreds or thousands of employees will be proud of.

The Key Attributes of a Unifying Goal

Any organisation can find and implement a unifying goal to initiate collaboration across their organisation utilising these four key concepts:

Qualitative

A unifying goal is not a KPI, a growth or financial statistic. The goal may well have objectives that lead to those results, but a unifying goal is a qualitative, compelling and worthwhile achievement that people are inspired to be part of.

Beware of goals that backfire because they are not consistent with your organisation's purpose and the value it creates for others—or goals that are not compelling or worthwhile to your people.

Shared

A unifying goal applies to every member of the executive team and flows down to their people who will need to collaborate in some way to achieve it. Everyone on the executive team must be accountable for the goal, they must be invested weekly and contribute ideas, resources and energy.

Important Situation

A Unifying Goal addresses an important situation. Important situations make unifying goals easy to define. It will be something that puts the enemy, competitor or problem in front of everyone in your organisation and inspires them to work together to change the situation.

Timeline

A Unifying Goal must have a timeline with an end date. The timeline is usually within a 12-month period period, (unless we are going to the moon). This brings urgency, accountability and energy to the goal. Objectives will be broken down into results and metrics with their own deadlines that serve the unifying goal.

STEP 2: ENSURE CLEAR ROLES, RESPONSIBILITIES & AUTONOMY

When every member of the executive team owns the unifying goal, the teams under them will start to take ownership for their parts of the goal. Objectives will be defined to meet the goal. Tasks will be broken down and given to teams who are involved in achieving each objective.

Cross-functional objectives must have one owner, instead of multiple managers or committees being responsible, one individual needs to own the completion of a single objective. There can be numerous people in numerous teams who are accountable to the owner of the objective by delivering their parts.

Each team must define what they need from other teams to deliver their part. These roles and responsibilities should be agreed, and progress monitored. The concept that if you're not serving the customer, you should be serving someone who is, relates to the people who depend on you to deliver their part—they are your customer. Service level agreements (SLAs) are a simple way to agree the responsibilities of one team to another.

However, they need to be realistic. For example, the IT department serves every department in an organisation, but they can't give everyone priority with their limited budget and resources. For this reason, SLAs need to come with concessions.

Concessions are where one department takes a hit to help another have a win. Software organisations often do this. One app team will make a financial loss for the product team being able to sell the end product at a profit. This is made simpler by reviewing how incentives are structured (in Step 3).

Finally, autonomy and decision-making authority is essential. In a collaborative environment, major decisions around the overall unifying goal are often made at the top. However, when roles and responsibilities are given to people lower down, these people need to be given autonomy to deliver their parts. This means allowing them to make decisions within their area of expertise and responsibility. They should not have to seek approval from above for things they are responsible for. In many organisations this means decentralising decisions at certain levels to accelerate collaboration and productivity.

It also means leveraging the power of hands-on leaders. Their expertise and connections to people, products, customers and other functional areas allow them to meaningfully engage in the work underway below them. It also positions them to collaborate with other functional areas during cross-team decision-making. This puts the decision-making power in the hands of people qualified to make the decision.

STEP 3: SHARED INCENTIVES

Start-ups often have highly collaborative teams. They think and behave more like owners than employees. There are three elements that, when combined, create this level of commitment:

1. A shared goal they believe in and work together to achieve
2. The autonomy to achieve the goal
3. Equity and reward if they are successful

Studies reveal[15] that once a meaningful shared goal is in place, there is a need for both autonomy and reward. Offering one and not the other has little effect on engagement and therefore performance. So, if you give people extra responsibility and autonomy to achieve a goal but without the upside of reward it has little impact on engagement. And if you only give a reward but no additional authority to achieve it there is also little effect on engagement. But when organisations give people the authority with an upside reward there is significantly higher (50% more) engagement than in organisations that do not offer both.

In Step 1 we covered the shared goal. In Step 2 we covered responsibility and autonomy. Now in Step 3 let's outline a simple approach to ensure incentives support collaboration. Shared goals need shared incentives.

Everyone would agree that compensation should be directly linked with performance. It sounds simple, right? But how to do you make sure that top-performing individuals are rewarded for their own performance but also motivated to collaborate with others to achieve the organisation's shared goal?

We want to avoid encouraging individuals and departments to act in their self-interest to achieve their part without working with others to achieve the bigger picture. The solution to this is a simple scorecard.

Once departments and teams are assigned to deliver objectives to achieve the unifying goal a scorecard can be created. The scorecard can include metrics and bonus incentives on 3 levels.

Level 1
The first level is the overall achievement of the unifying goal. If the organisation achieves it, then a percentage of the bonus is paid.

Level 2
The second level is each team delivering their parts to the other teams who depend on them—their customers.

Level 3
The third level is individual performance on their tasks. A cross-team component can be added to show they contributed to solving problems or added value to the objectives on their scorecard with other teams.

Every employee's scorecard would be matched to their role and team's contribution to the assigned objectives, their customer and the overall unifying goal. Their bonus or rewards would be commensurate with their role and contribution. For example, if a new product was being developed and then taken to market, salespeople would earn direct commission on individual sales for year 1, product development people might get a trailing commission on the new product's sales and internal functions like IT, Legal and Finance could share in a pool of profits for doing their part in supporting other departments to meet their objectives in designing, building and selling the product.

Setting the Incentive Amounts

When I worked at SAP in the early days, we were one of the first organisations not to cap rewards and bonuses. We linked rewards to achievement. One year a salesperson made more money in sales commissions than the CEO of SAP America's total package. Another year a consulting director made over $1m when the average package back then was around $250k. This sent a clear message to employees that meant: "We believe you can make a big difference to our business. We don't want to limit your performance, so we won't limit your upside".

Meanwhile, many other organisations I consulted to had small bonuses of 10%-20% that were capped. The message this sent to employees was: "We only think you can make a 10% difference". Employees didn't often exceed these low expectations.

It takes effort to balance the budget, break up the objectives and define the scorecards. Shared incentives can be a complex subject, but it doesn't have to be that complicated with a top-down approach to simplify incentives by removing conflicts and rewarding everyone around the shared goal and their part in collaborating to achieve it.

Simplifying existing incentives to remove conflicts is an important and essential start. This can be done by:

- Removing conflicting KPI's between teams
- Evaluating whether a function even needs a P&L
- Allow people to focus on great customer service rather than the P&L
- Sharing budget or resources with other teams without penalty for the bigger picture outcome

These are a few examples of removing unnecessary conflicts that undermine collaboration and support the achievement of an organisation's overall goals.

With conflicts removed, creating a scorecard with 3 levels as simple as possible is easy to achieve with some consulting advice or a dedicated internal team. The return on investment here is well worth the effort.

STEP 4: REGULAR COORDINATION ON PROGRESS

As discussed, the approach to creating a collaborative environment is based on the timeless discipline of project management. Projects have regular meetings (often weekly) with team leaders to track progress, discuss problems and collaborate on solutions.

Running an entire organisation this way is no different. High-tech firms, engineering firms, consumer product firms and many others have a project management approach to bringing new products to market. The well-known ones like Facebook, Apple and Microsoft are constantly running projects both for new products and for existing BAU goals.

Once your organisation has the components of a unifying goal (with objectives allocated to different teams and functions), clear roles and responsibilities to each other with autonomy to achieve their parts and with aligned incentives, it is easy to manage progress and to identify and deal with problems. People who do not collaborate become obvious. Teams that fall behind can be focused on and supported. It is an exciting environment having everyone working together, being rewarded together and reaching for success together.

An inside view of Apple

Apple is one of the best examples of collaboration in the high-performing organisations studied. Their executive team meets weekly to track progress, discuss problems and collaborate on solutions. Because there is good collaboration at the top of the organisation, it flows down and out from that meeting to the many teams working together on the bigger picture and unifying goal.

One of the things that makes executives at Apple more effective at collaborating is knowledge of their function and those around them. They are hands-on managers who have expertise in their direct function, as well as an appreciation and understanding of how other departments function and how they integrate to work together.

A year before Steve Jobs died, Walt Mossberg of the Wall Street Journal interviewed Jobs about how his highly secretive organisation worked. What Jobs revealed was leadership and organisational GOLD.

Here's the transcript of Jobs speaking off the cuff:

"One of the keys to Apple is (that) Apple is an incredibly collaborative company...We are organised like a start-up; one person is in charge of iPhone OS software; one person is in charge of Mac hardware; one person is in charge of iPhone hardware engineering; another person is in charge of worldwide marketing another person is in charge of operations...we're organised like a startup. We're the biggest startup on the planet...

...we all meet for three hours once a week and we talk about everything we're doing (in) the whole business... there's tremendous teamwork at the top of the company which filters down to tremendous teamwork throughout the company...teamwork is dependent on trusting the other folks to come with their part without watching them all the time but trusting that they're going to come through with their parts and that's what we do really well and we're great at figuring out how to divide things up into these great teams that we have and all work on the same thing, touch bases frequently and bring it all together into a product.

We do that really well and so what I do all day is meet with teams of people and work on ideas and solve problems to make new products, to make new marketing programs, whatever it is (we are working on as a priority or strategic goal at Apple)".

Jobs' comments reveal a purposeful approach to working together on shared goals from the top of the organisation down. They also revealed how hands-on he was. Even though he was not technical, he had good overall domain knowledge of every team.

The same is true of all leaders at Apple. They are all hands-on. Years earlier, Jobs removed all general managers who didn't have domain expertise and replaced them with functional leaders who had domain expertise and would be hands-on with their teams and had an understanding and ability to collaborate with other teams to produce an end result.

Your organisation can replicate this approach

Every project manager in every industry has domain knowledge of the various teams on the project. A builder will have domain knowledge of every tradesperson on a building site: plumbers, concreters, electricians etc.

The "CEO as project manager" of the entire organisation is no different. They may have a Chief Operating Officer (COO) or Chief Transformation Officer (CTO) spanning every department, but the hands-on CEO will be involved in every team to ensure collaboration, to act as a tie breaker and to push for and contribute ideas.

This is a great opportunity for CEOs to drive change and performance in the operation. Traditionally, executives drive operations while the CEO leads only a small group of people. This limits the CEOs ability to influence the very thing they are ultimately responsible for: overall operational performance.

However, using this approach of "CEO as project manager", the CEO gets to set the unifying goal, define the objectives and have their executive team work together, report on and be accountable for progress.

STEP 5: MEASURE & IMPROVE COLLABORATION EFFECTIVENESS

Measure

To fully leverage collaboration, it needs to be measured. Setting incentive scorecards is one step. The other is to continue assessing the organisation for hidden obstacles.

Your organisation can use a number of existing assessments or use the tool created for this book, the 5 Factor Assessment. Either way, a commitment to collaboration requires a commitment to ongoing measurement of performance and obstacles.

Improve

The final step is to act on the measurement. If obstacles are uncovered, they must be addressed. If people are not collaborating, the cause must be addressed, and people coached or moved.

The Bottom Line

Collaboration is the key to achieving high performance and results from a good strategy.

It is not enough to hire smart people, put them together and expect results. They will eventually get stuck. The environment you create that shapes their behaviour is everything.

Increasing collaboration by creating a collaborative environment isn't as complicated or difficult as it might appear.

Setting clear goals, responsibilities, incentives and committing to open communication, mutual respect and making changes as you go is the answer.

When I was at SAP our marketing byline read: "The best run companies run SAP". While automation (and SAP) software helps organisations run more effectively, I believe the best run companies **know how to work together.**

If you want different results, you need to do things differently. Following the lead of the world's high-performing organisations in a way that suits your organisation is a great place to start.

A final note on the final factor:

The fifth factor, Cross-Team Collaboration, is dependent on solid execution of the first four factors. Highly collaborative teams need *Hands-on* leaders who are involved, have domain knowledge, contribute and foster debate and ideas from everyone. They need a *Purpose-Led* culture that gives them a reason beyond achieving numbers to commit to. Something they don't just have to do, but that they want to do. They need a focus on *Customer-Centricity* to allow them to focus on delivering for their customer (the internal team in the chain waiting on them to deliver, or the external end customer), without conflicting internal KPIs or demands from above. And finally, people want and need to be *Fully Empowered* with clear direction, expectations, know-how, tools, trust, autonomy and accountability to deliver their part in a fun and cohesive environment. None of these things can be achieved without the others.

The first four factors combined with creating a project environment are without doubt how I have seen the highest-performing teams operate. And it is how many of the world's high-performing organisations produce the exceptional results they enjoy.

COVID-19 brought a change to leadership in many organisations. Some leaders shifted from command-and-control to coaching high-performing teams.

Many CEOs and leaders reported feeling energised by leading through the crisis. Things got real. They had to communicate more regularly on a real level with everyone; they built trust, and their actions were filled with purpose and meaning.

These leaders broke down boundaries and silos, streamlined decisions, empowered front-line workers and inspired people to get things done in a fraction of the time. Because of the pandemic, leaders acted as visionaries instead of commanders. They empowered and coached people, embraced change and collaboration, and created engagement with a shared purpose that lifted productivity. New technology rolled out in days not months, products went from prototype to production in a week instead of a year. Shit got real. And shit got done.

Many learned that things could happen faster and with greater purpose. To maintain the speed, collaboration, purpose, simplicity and results achieved in the pandemic, leaders can make permanent structural and operational changes that inspire and engage people to be more efficient and innovative. But first they need to continue leading with authenticity and purpose that connects with people.

Becoming Unstuck!

Shifting your organisation into high-performance means change. There is good change and bad change. Large change management programs that create uncertainty, fear and a sense of losing control are bad change.

The themes outlined in this book are good change: retaining your current structure; creating more certainty by providing clearer purpose and direction; alignment on goals and incentives; becoming more hands-on and connected to vital knowledge; and empowering people with autonomy and accountability. This kind of change can unlock immediate cost and time efficiencies, and a willingness to adopt change, collaborate, and get results on the shared goals and reasons behind them.

All that is required is ACTION. Reading a business book without acting on it is entertaining but won't get results. It's time to take action and get results.

Let's get started. You're not alone. This next section is your roadmap, coach, consultant and guide.

21
A Leader's Roadmap

This is your suggested roadmap for implementing the 5 Factors to achieve high performance, results and the achievement of a unifying goal.

Some consultants will say you need to invest now to gain rewards later. This means it will hurt before it gets better. I am not one of those consultants. The approach outlined in this book is cost neutral and designed to generate results immediately, but at a pace that works for your organisation.

The approach in this book is NOT a big bang, once-off event. Many dramatic change programs fail. This approach is an iterative, low-risk, high-return approach. It is intended to produce sustained results.

The Suggested Roadmap

This roadmap marks a logical journey from a START with points along the way. It can be adapted to suit you, your organisation and your resources.

START - Decide to change

Working harder is not the path to high performance. Most organisations do not suffer from inaction. They are already working harder than ever. The problem is not lack of action; it is often the wrong action. It is normal for organisations to follow established thinking and behaviours. After all, that is what created success. But when conditions change, the things that previously created success can create failure.

Speeding up the wrong action exhausts resources and digs a deeper hole. *The first rule of holes: When you are in one, stop digging.*[1] All organisations reach a point where they need to do things differently. History is littered with leaders and organisations that failed because they didn't change. The 5 Factors make change easier by providing insight, inspiration and alignment. First, decide to change.

1 - Revise and publish a meaningful purpose

Become hands-on. Lead with the influence of a founder. To do this, start with Chapter 3 Get out into the Field. Once you have made connections in the field, gained essential insights to help you; learned about obstacles and passions and earned greater influence with people, it is time to work on Chapter 7 Creating Your Organisation's Purpose.

1 Molly Ivins

2 - Set a clear goal

With a well-accepted and inspiring purpose, it is time to focus everyone on a unifying goal. This is the goal that addresses the most *important situation* you face right now. Revisit your favourite parts from Factor #3 Customer-Centricity, to ensure the order of starting with the customer and working backwards. This will help inform your unifying goal.

Next, revisit the part of Chapter 20 Creating a Collaborative Environment that outlines how to set a unifying goal. You will come back to the rest of that chapter later, but for now just focus on the creation of a unifying goal.

3 - Assess your organisation's strengths and weaknesses

It is important to identify how your organisation is doing on the Factors. How does your organisation score? Where are the obstacles, gaps and opportunities? Some obstacles could be your leaders, your people, your culture or your processes. Once you have this data you can develop targeted solutions.

You can use your own assessment, or the 5 Factor Assessment Tool developed for this book, to gather accurate data on your organisation.

4 - Send an Invitation to Change

Start the process to get everyone onboard with the Unifying Goal and to leverage the 5 Factors to accelerate performance and results (see Chapter 24).

5 - Get the right people on the bus

Borrowing a term from Jim Collins' book Good to Great, you need to "get the right people on the bus" early in this journey.

The 5 Factor organisations have hands-on leaders at their core. They are connected to their people, operation and customers. They have domain expertise in the functional units that report up to them. They're not general managers who manage only to metrics. This leads to a narrow focus on numbers without an appreciation of the impact on products, people, customers and the organisation's overall strategic goals. The difference in performance between hands-on leaders and old-style general managers is significant.

It is reasonable to expect leaders to have expertise and domain knowledge beyond an ability to manage numbers. This is particularly important in areas of emerging technology and social trends that impact business decisions. It is also imperative for cross-team collaboration to have domain expertise wide enough to collaborate with other parts of the business.

The assessment will reveal some changes you need to make in leadership. Some of these changes can be made with education, workshops and coaching for Factor 1: Hands-On Leadership and skills from Factor 4: Fully Empowered People.

Other changes may result in moving people in and out of leadership roles, including senior leaders. The 5 Factor Assessment will provide insights not normally available to a CEO, board, executive team and those below.

Once the unifying goal and culture are set, it will become clear which people cannot, or will not do their part in delivering on the unifying goal, be that through lack of expertise, willingness or cultural fit. Often people will choose to leave or move, but if they don't it is important to get the right people on (and off) the bus early in this process.

6 - Focus on the most important things

You can't address all obstacles, gaps and opportunities at the same time. Consistent with the approach in this book, simplify efforts by placing focus on areas with the biggest impact and lowest effort. In a consulting workshop, you could map these on a graph with four quadrants to arrive at the best areas and ideas that have both high impact and low effort. It needs facilitation to help stakeholders arrive at consensus. The result you should aim for is rapid alignment and focus.

7 - Empower people

Once you have a unifying goal, a project environment and well-defined responsibilities identifying who will do which parts to achieve the goal, it is time to empower people. Give people more autonomy and decision-making authority; reduce the number of steps, meetings, decision levels etc., to increase speed, ownership and output. Revisit Factor #4 to select the actions you believe will suit your organisation around empowering people and removing unnecessary obstacles.

8 - Encourage collaboration

With a meaningful purpose, a unifying goal, and an understanding of the obstacles, gaps and opportunities to leverage the factors, it is time to leverage the power of collaboration in a way that gets results. Revisit Factor #5 Cross-Team Collaboration. Avoid the common challenges by removing conflicting goals and incentives that create silos, shift the culture by making it safe, extend trust and simplify by subtracting rather than adding meetings, emails and activities.

Create psychological safety that makes people comfortable in admitting they have a problem, need help or want to suggest a change to how something is done. Create a culture of working together to solve problems rather than assigning blame. Identify barriers and work together to remove them.

RINSE AND REPEAT

Return to Step 2 to create a new unifying goal once this one is complete. Repeat the process again for your next unifying goal. Create a cycle of continuous improvement to sustain performance and avoid adding future complexity and obstacles or becoming complacent and slipping into old patterns.

The Bottom Line

Your success in becoming unstuck, improving performance and accelerating results will come by:

- Assessing your organisation on the 5 Factors
- Getting the right people on the bus
- Creating a meaningful purpose
- Setting a unifying goal
- Becoming more hands-on at all levels
- Focussing on the most important things
- Empowering people
- Encouraging collaboration and
- Fostering a culture of learning and problem-solving where the best ideas win

These principles can be applied to any organisation to increase performance and generate better results faster.

22
Using Consultants

It is possible to implement the 5 Factors without big consulting budgets, complex change programs and huge investments in time and effort that distract your business. Having said that, you will likely need consultants to help. It's how you use consultants that is important.

There is work that you and your people must do. And there is work that consultants can do. You cannot outsource culture or behavioural change. If you want people to commit, you must show commitment. You must lead this change.

You can't use consultants to write your purpose or to choose and enthuse the workforce with a unifying goal. You need to be hands-on to earn trust, influence and create engagement from everyone below you. Consultants cannot and should not do that for you. This is not something you can outsource.

Your people must also own their part. Your people know their business better than consultants and should be responsible for any changes and improvements.

Amazon do not use consultants in their "working backwards" design sessions. Amazon employees collaborate from different departments to design products based on their experience of customer needs.

Flight attendants, mechanics and other staff at Southwest Airlines work together to review customer feedback and decide on actions to improve service. This is their business, and they know it best.

For sustained, repeatable high performance you and your people must own the input, the ideas and make the changes yourselves.

Consultants can assist with the following roles and tasks:

- Measuring and reporting on your organisation's 5 Factor scores
- Facilitating the process to implement the 5 Factors.
- Setting up a Project Management Office to implement your unifying goal
- Using tools and forums to collect input from your people to:
- Map internal customer service levels
- Identify unnecessary obstacles and complexity standing in the way of speed and results
- Gather and collate new ideas to improve performance
- Run group workshops for leaders and their teams

- Executive Coaching for Hands-on leadership techniques
- Challenging, supporting and keeping the team on track

Consultants can be effective by providing resources, perspective and external skills to allow you and your team to focus on the changes and direction you need to take. Using consultants in this way will lower your consulting spend, allow your people to share the depth of their experience in your business and increase their ownership, control and accountability.

23

Finding Time to Lead

Many CEOs and executives find it difficult to find time to lead. They are time-poor and overwhelmed with data, emails, meetings, management reporting and/or board responsibilities. On top of this, they own the strategy and culture and need to be responsive to direct reports and high-priority business situations. It doesn't leave much time to do some of the things that 5 Factor Organisations seem to do, like being hands-on with the operation, employees and customers while driving a unifying goal.

Yet some CEOs and executive leaders seem to find time. One who was famous for the impact of his leadership was Steve Jobs, CEO of Apple. He was involved in many aspects of Apple as well as being the front man. He found time to articulate and constantly drive Apple's vision and strategy, he was involved in all of Apple's main projects and even small but important product design decisions.

Jobs had a different view on where he and his people spent their time. He once famously said:

"People think focus means saying yes to the thing you've got to focus on. But that's not what it means at all. It means saying no to the hundred other (things) that there are. You have to pick carefully". [25]

He created focus by getting the team together at the start of the year, brainstorming a list of the top objectives, then reducing the list of 10. Then he would cut the list to just 3 things so they could focus everything on them for faster, better results. This still meant dozens of projects underneath those 3 objectives, but it was a lot less than his teams initially wanted to focus on. This is one of the ways he saved Apple from bankruptcy and grew it into the biggest organisation on the planet. He cut the number of products and projects his employees were focused on so they could achieve the ones that made a big impact.

Here are some ideas to consider to create time to lead:

1. Give yourself permission to simplify and focus. Stop adding and start subtracting. Buck the trend to add projects, initiatives and goals, and start subtracting.

2. Reduce the number of strategic objectives you and your people focus on this year. Choose the ones with the greatest impact, giving you and your people the best chance to focus on and achieve them. At some point, the more you try to do, the less you get done

3. Re-establish the objectives of every recurring meeting in your calendar. Cut some meetings and choose not to attend others.

4. Use hands-on leadership all the way down the organisation. Set clear expectations and accountability, then delegate authority. Remove some approvals from your list. Trust people to do their jobs. Check on them. Hold them accountable. Manage by exception.

5. Condense 1:1 meetings and daily interruptions into a daily open-door meeting at the same time every morning. Invite people to attend to raise issues. Attendance is optional. People are encouraged to bring up items they need help with. Then during the day, rather than interrupt you or send an email, they are encouraged to wait until tomorrow's meeting unless it is urgent and can't wait.

6. Use an executive coach to help you find ideas that are specific to you and your organisation.

24
Send an Invitation to Change

The *Invitation to Change* is an example of using your personal power versus control to inspire change. What is the difference between power and control?

Power can magnify and accelerate results. Control can restrict and slow results. Most of this book has been about leveraging personal power to lead and inspire; to set expectations and support people to achieve them; and to remove controls that restrict people's creativity, common sense and willingness to try harder and to work together.

Control is often an anxiety response. When we fear a potential outcome, such as people doing the wrong thing, we try to control things. Some controls make sense, but over time organisations have become stuck under decades of controls and bureaucracy designed to control things. This makes it extremely difficult for leaders to effect genuine, "Holy-crap, how-did-they-do-that?" outcomes. Sure, you can do deals like outsourcing and mergers but that isn't the kind of industry- and people-changing outcomes this book is about.

SpaceX didn't create the world's largest satellite constellation to provide high-speed internet across the planet with excessive controls on their people's ability to achieve such an outcome. Your organisation might not be changing the world like SpaceX, but it might have an ability to lead its industry with new outcomes that excite customers, investors and employees.

If you want to generate higher performance and exceptional outcomes, it is time to try something different. Instead of control, you must be brave enough to trust people in a smart way that sets clear expectations, gives them control and holds them accountable. If some of them break your trust, you have the power to remove the offenders without adding controls that punish everyone else, and get in the way of your goals.

The power of sending an invitation to change comes from your ability to encourage people to willingly engage in change.

As Tony Robbins once said, "Engaging people is about meeting their needs not yours." Not meeting the needs of those who need to change is a form of control not personal power. Not meeting people's needs is one of the biggest mistakes that change programs make over and over, year after year.

Let's be honest: nobody likes change, and yet we choose it all the time. We change our cars, we move houses, we change jobs. It's fine when we want to change but if someone forces those changes on us, we don't like it.

Most people I have spoken to about change management in their company cringe at the very mention of it. This is because change was done to them, not with them. The easiest change is the change we choose. When change has a reason, benefits, a degree of certainty and choice, we are far more likely to want it.

Great leadership starts with great communication. Great communication is authentic. It shows under-standing and empathy for those receiving it and is well-structured and done with care. The structure below is intended for you to adapt and use in your own voice and style.

To show how the structure works, I have included step-by-step instructions with an example at each step.

Writing Your Invitation to Change

1. Start by announcing "Why change needs to happen" in a way that people can personally relate to. This requires your communication to engage both rational and emotional thinking. Great communication engages people's hearts and minds.

Here's an example email:
Our company was built on a desire to provide [INSERT YOUR PURPOSE e.g. the best premium airline experience in Australia]. Our success was earned, but it is not a privilege. It is something we need

*to earn every day. [OUTLINE YOUR
IMPORTANT SITUATION, e.g. Our business has
been affected by global events, increased competition,
and a need to rebuild trust in our brand]. This means
changing the way we work together to benefit
everyone: you, our customers, our shareholders and our
partners.*

2. Next, explain that everyone will have input into
any changes and why this is important.

*Your input and opinions are essential to this change.
While the executive team is ultimately responsible for
our strategy, we need and want your input. You know
more about your part of our business than anyone else.
And it is only right that you have input into any
change that affects you and our joint success.*

*The only thing I ask is that your input is given in
good faith with a positive intent to benefit everyone.
We all get frustrated but can use that to come up with
great ideas. So, if your input is initially negative,
please turn it into a constructive idea – it could be
quite valuable to all of us. That doesn't mean you have
to agree with how we do things now, you can certainly
disagree, but offer constructive alternatives. That is
the input I need from you.*

*Everyone's input is welcome. Everyone's opinion
matters. Be assured there are no such things as dumb
ideas. Every idea you provide will be listened to and
considered.*

3. Explain there will be two kinds of change, the goal of the change and the benefits to them:

> *We need to make two changes to the way we work. The first kind of change is to agree what we are all focused on. At present we all have so many different goals and priorities. To help simplify the demands on all of us we are going back to basics. We are going to focus on an important goal that applies to every one of us.*
>
> *[INSERT UNIFYING GOAL, e.g. the Qantas Unifying goal is:*
> *Our #1 goal is to restore our customers' trust in us. We will make it easier and fairer for our customers to interact with our people and our systems to book flights, use points, check-in, fly with confidence and be treated with genuine care and respect they deserve in the Spirit of Australia that defines our airline and our country.]*
>
> *Everyone has a part to play in this. Everyone has ideas and a contribution to make. To achieve our goal, we have several objectives that range from [INSERT SOME OF THE OBJECTIVES to OTHER OBJECTIVES]. You will have input into them, a role to play, and be rewarded on our joint success.*
>
> *The second kind of change in how we work is to remove unnecessary conflicts, overlap and obstacles. We need to improve and streamline our day-to-day operation.*

We want to achieve three things here:

1. To make our customer experience easier, faster and more enjoyable.
2. To make your experience at work easier, faster and more enjoyable.
3. To save time, effort and money to invest in these improvements.

I am sure you are doing things that are obsolete, slow or unnecessarily difficult that could be improved. For example (include some of what you learned in the field).
We need to improve, innovate and reinvent the way we do business. We need to do this to stay relevant with what our customers want, how technology and business are changing and to offer a better experience than anyone else.

Explain why this is better than cutting costs, budgets and perks:

To find efficiencies in time, effort and money many organisations would start by cutting jobs and budgets. We would rather start by cutting unnecessary work, processes, or rules that waste time and money and demotivate you from doing your best work. In choosing what to remove and change, we need to stay compliant, and we need to stay safe. Rest assured our goal is to streamline our day-to-day operation while improving our customer and employee experience so that we can achieve our goal of [INSERT unifying goal].

Close by stating your intentions: This builds trust and shows you are real. Use your own voice, but here is an example to help you:

Finally, on a personal note I want you all to know where I am coming from. I believe that life is precious, and work should enrich your life. Work should be fun and challenging. It should be financially and personally rewarding. And should be doing good work you are proud of.

I also believe that we should take our work seriously but not take ourselves too seriously. Let's take pride, have fun and work hard to continue earning our success with the great service we provide.

Explain when and how to make it predictable and more certain for them:

We will not be doing this as one big change. We will take the time to do it over the coming year. You will be contacted and invited to participate and provide your input over the coming weeks and months.

Naturally we will need to prioritise all the ideas we collect. We will keep you updated on the which of your suggested ideas and changes we will do first, second and

so on. And if we can't do some of them, we will also let
you know.
  I look forward to the great things we can do together
with purpose and pride.

Jane or John Doe
CEO

When you sit down to write this in your own voice, remember this is just an invitation. It is not a detailed change plan with all of the details, dates and actions. Those will come.

It is crucial that you do what you say you are going to do. Most people today are cynical and have heard all of this before. You have a chance to win the trust of your people by following through. So there needs to be visible actions to follow.

Your Project Management Office (PMO) or project manager will execute the process for collecting and managing this and reporting up to the executive team weekly, or within the timelines you agree to.

25
How Does Your Organisation Score?

You can measure how your organisation scores on the 5 Factors. The 5 Factor Assessment Model of Execution (F.A.M.E.) was developed to measure how well an organisation is executing. It will assess your organisation for opportunities to improve execution.

The Assessment Report
The executive sponsor will receive a tailored and confidential report for the organisation. The report details scores across leader, department and geography, with an interpretation of the scores, an analysis of the highest areas of impact, and summary recommendations.

F.A.M.E.

FIVE-FACTOR MODEL OF EXECUTION

Assessment Summary Report
By Mike Alafaci

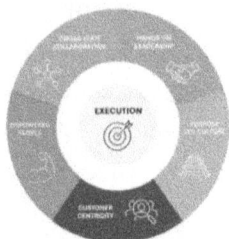

Prepared For:	Your Organisation Pty Ltd
Executive Sponsor:	Your Name
Assessment Date:	10th April 2025

Scores and Recommendations

Scores and recommendations are given at organisation, leader, regional and department levels.

Organisation Level Scores

The example score below shows the organisation's total score for all 5 Factors.

Your Organisation's Total Score

71%

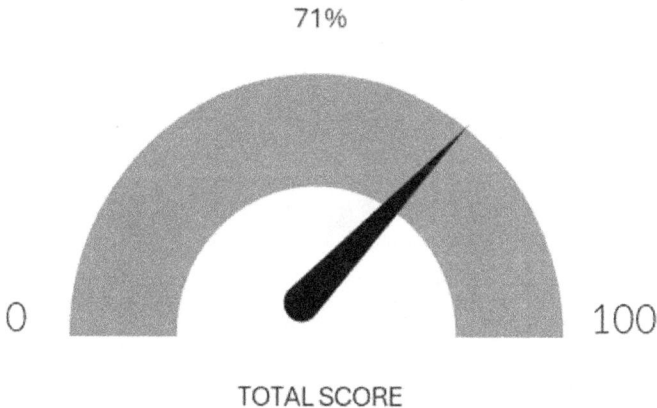

0   100

TOTAL SCORE

Factor Level Scores

The total score is then broken down into a score for each factor.

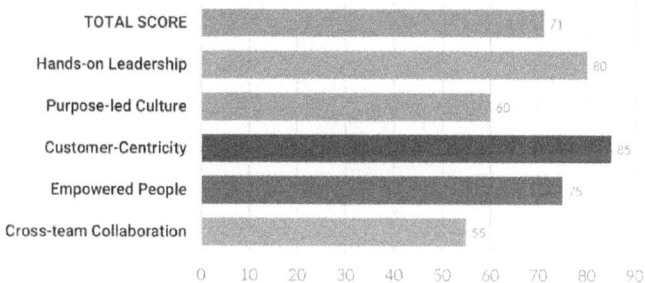

TOTAL SCORE	71
Hands-on Leadership	80
Purpose-led Culture	60
Customer-Centricity	85
Empowered People	75
Cross-team Collaboration	55

Element Level Scores

Each Factor contains elements and their scores. The example below for Factor #2 Purpose-Led Culture reveals that this organisation has a reasonably well-**articulated** purpose (score of 70), however its purpose could be more **meaningful** (score 60) and it could be better **integrated** into decisions and operation (score 50).

Factor #2 Purpose-led Culture

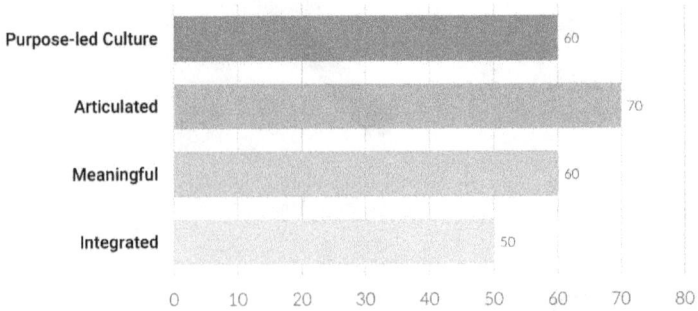

Leader, Department and Regional Level Scores

Scores on each factor can be customised and shown at Leadership Level.

FACTOR SCORES AT LEADER LEVEL

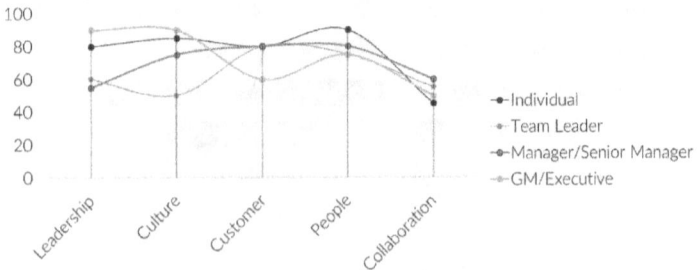

Scores can be broken out by Department Level.

FACTOR SCORES AT DEPARTMENT LEVEL

Scores can be broken out by Regional or Geographic Level.

FACTOR SCORES AT REGIONAL/GEOGRAPHIC LEVEL

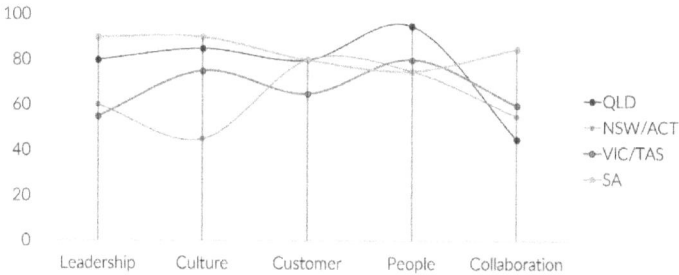

Almost every organisation can benefit from discovering what and who is holding it back from achieving results faster.

To inquire about an assessment for your organisation Email the author at: mike@mikealafaci.com

Notes:

1.Three NPS lessons to learn from Amazon.
https://customergauge.com/benchmarks/blog/3-nps-lessons-to-learn-from-amazon

2.Why IT Projects Still Fail
https://www.cio.com/article/230427/why-it-projects-still-fail.html

3. Voluntary employee turnover has risen year-on-year for the last decade, according to the U.S. Bureau of Labor Statistics.
https://www.linkedin.com/pulse/how-apple-retains-90-its-employees-spoiler-through-training-edume

4. Management behaviors that foster employee engagement by Paul J. Zak, Feb 2017
https://hbr.org/2017/01/the-neuroscience-of-trust#:~:text=Compared with people at low,lives, 40% less burnout.

5.Purpose-driven organisations and 2.5 times more effective at innovation.
https://hbr.org/2023/05/organize-your-change-initiative-around-purpose-and-benefits

6. CEOs last to know why organisation is stuck.
https://hbr.org/2017/08/what-we-learned-about-bureaucracy-from-7000-hbr-readers

7. 'Why did Nokia fail and what can you learn from it?'
https://medium.com/multiplier-magazine/why-did-nokia-fail-81110d981787

8. 50 Stats That Prove The Value Of Customer Experience. Forbes 2019.
https://customergauge.com/benchmarks/blog/3-nps-lessons-to-learn-from-amazon

9. What went wrong at Boeing? Forbes 2013.
https://www.forbes.com/sites/stevedenning/2013/01/21/what-went-wrong-at-boeing/?sh=1cb3e08f7b1b

10. Having a clear purpose drives performance. IESE December 1, 2020.
https://www.iese.edu/insight/articles/clear-purpose-drives-performance/

11. For Corporate Purpose to Matter, You've Got to Measure It. August 16, 2018.
https://www.bcg.com/publications/2018/corporate-purpose-to-matter-measure-it

12. What makes power hungry bosses tick? And what can be done about it? August 23, 2022.
https://www.unsw.edu.au/newsroom/news/2022/08/what-makes-power-hungry-bosses-tick--and-what-can-be-done-about-

13. What successful Purpose Statements Do Differently. March 01, 2024.
https://hbr.org/2024/03/what-successful-purpose-statements-do-differently

14. Purpose At Work: How Starbucks Scales Impact By Listening To All The Stakeholders In Our Shared Future. July 7, 2021. Forbes.
https://www.forbes.com/sites/simonmainwaring/2021/07/07/purpose-at-work-how-starbucks-scales-impact-by-listening-to-all-the-stakeholders-in-our-shared-future/?sh=1885a7c95bfc

15. Does Linking Worker Pay to Firm Performance Help the Best Firms Do Even Better? January 2012. Douglas L. Kruse, Joseph R. Blasi & Richard B. Freeman.
https://www.nber.org/papers/w17745

16. Former Boeing Engineers Say Relentless Cost-Cutting Sacrificed Safety. May, 2019.
https://www.bloomberg.com/news/features/2019-05-09/former-boeing-engineers-say-relentless-cost-cutting-sacrificed-safety?embedded-checkout=true

17. Boeing: Oops we did it again. Ted M. January 31, 2024.
https://www.linkedin.com/pulse/boeing-oops-we-did-again-ted-mckinney-ph-d--gxcxf/

18. Elon Musk Just Taught Hands-On Leadership In 51 Seconds. Rachel Wells. Sep 3, 2023. Forbes. Rachel Wells
https://www.forbes.com/sites/rachelwells/2023/09/03/elon-musk-just-taught-hands-on-leadership-in-51-seconds/#

19. Elon Musk and productivity. Gustavo Garza. LinkedIn Article.April 21, 2018
https://www.linkedin.com/pulse/elon-musk-productivity-gustavo-garza/

20. How Apple Is Organized for Innovation. HBR Magazine November-December, 2020.
https://hbr.org/2020/11/how-apple-is-organized-for-innovation.

21. The Real Leadership Lessons of Steve Jobs. Walter Issacson. HBR Magazine. April, 2012.
https://hbr.org/2012/04/the-real-leadership-lessons-of-steve-jobs#:~:text=There%20was%20a%20stunned%20silence,and%20it's%20true%20for%20products.".

22. How Microsoft, Lendlease and Virgin changed their culture. Patrick Durkin and Sally Pattern. Australian Financial Review. Feb 15, 2024.

23. 15 Years ago today, Steve Jobs wrote an Open Letter to 'All iPhone Customers.' It's a Masterclass in Admitting When You're Wrong. Jason Aten. September 6, 2022. Inc. Australia.
https://www.inc-aus.com/jason-aten/15-years-ago-today-steve-jobs-wrote-an-open-letter-to-all-iphone-customers-its-a-mastercala-in-admitting-when-youre-wrong.html

24. Chris Ziegler. Nokia P: N97 taught company some tough lessons. Fed, 2010.
https://www.engadget.com/2010-02-23-nokia-vp-n97-taught-company-some-tough-lessons.html?_fsig=yXDTrODrPNRJCCjHKawFbg--%7EA

25. Brenhard Schroeder. Entrepreneurs and small business owners: Steve Jobs advice on saying no more often to achieve your goals. October 31, 2022. Forbes.
https://www.forbes.com/sites/bernhardschroeder/2022/10/31/entrepreneurs-and-small-business-owners-steve-jobs-advice-on-saying-no-more-often-to-achieve-your-goals/

26. Walt Mossberg and Kara Swisher. All Things Digital: D8 Conference 2010. Video content YouTube.
https://youtu.be/i5f8bqYYwps?si=OI6vuEHIgwIf6udS

27. The 4 Disciplines of Execution. Chris McChesney, Sean Covey, Jim Huling. Simon and Shuster 2012.

Acknowledgements

Any good leader has people in their life that they trust to mentor, advise and challenge them. I have some special people like this who I trust and value greatly. They helped me write this book by sharing stories, discussing ideas, challenging me and listening to me think out loud (a lot). I would like to thank them here.

The first person I want to thank is my wife, Mel Alafaci. You simply said one day, "You should write a book". Thank you for the encouragement. You got me started and you made sure I finished, but more on that later.

Once I decided to write a book, I quickly realised I didn't really know how despite having written thousands of emails, papers and reports. Two special people helped me find my way into book writing. Marie Alafaci, my cousin, published author and editor, thank you for your encouragement and help getting this book into shape. Bill O'Hanlon, author of over 40 books in the USA, thank you for your support, good writing vibes, teaching and friendship over the years.

A book like this shouldn't be written in isolation. It needs subject matter experts and businesspeople who can pressure test it.

John Grant, co-founder and past CEO of Data#3, client and now friend, thank you for your experience and perspective over many breakfasts and lunches; Jerry Maycock, past CEO and Chair of large Australian corporations like AGL, CSR and Transgrid, thank you for sharing your class and finesse both in big business and (unfortunately for me) on the golf course; Dan Pritchard startup CEO extraordinaire, you can get the best out of anyone including me, thank you for being you. Joel Palmer, past Australian Financial Review (AFR) Journalist & now financial advisor to large family offices, thank you for your perspective. Kirstin Ferguson, Australian author, leadership expert and super busy, inspirational woman, thank you for generously sharing your time, encouragement and insightful feedback.

Seamus Kirkpatrick, professional musician who knows more about corporate behaviour than most corporate people, thank you for all of the chats; Jim Katzenberger, Principal of The Accelerx Group in Pennsylvania, a brilliant business mind and friend, and the younger brother of Ken Katzenberger who this book is dedicated to. Thank you Jim! Ken lives on in this book and in our friendship. Nikki Stevens, a super professional consultant and organisation psychology registrar, thank you for keeping me moving and helping build and finesse the assessment tool that goes with this book.

Mark Prince, my best man and friend, thank you for getting me unstuck when I was outlining the book. You got involved at just the right time. And to all of my other friends who listened at one stage or another to my ideas, challenges and rantings. Thank you for being there when I needed you.

Lindy MacPherson my good friend. You give more than you take. As a well-respected senior business leader, you are a great example of what is in this book and this is reflected in every team you have led. One reason people trust and follow you is that you are almost always right when you assess a situation, team or individual—well at least the last 400 times I can remember. This takes more than keen observation skills; it takes the leadership skill of empathy. Thank you for your empathy, support, edits, chats and friendship. It meant a lot when you said after reading my initial outline, "Mike, I read a LOT of business books every year (23 last year!), I think you have something here. You should write this book".

As I write the final words in this book, I owe another thank you to my wife Mel. Over the years, you have patiently listened to me talk (a lot) about the good, the bad, the ugly and the exceptional leadership practices I have witnessed. But it takes more than talk to write a book. It takes action! And that is your strength. While I was writing this book, you wrote 5 cookbooks of your own. And then you made sure I finished writing this book. Thank you for your support, love and the way you care for everyone around you.

www.ingramcontent.com/pod-product-compliance
Lightning Source LLC
Chambersburg PA
CBHW030456210326
41597CB00013B/695